Solving Children's

Day-to-Day Problems

Ms Nivedita

•

Illustrations by:

Pritam Paul

UNICORN BOOKS

Publishers
UNICORN BOOKS

J-3/16 , Daryaganj, New Delhi-110002
☎ 23276539, 23272783, 23272784 • *Fax:* 011-23260518
E-mail: unicornbooks@vsnl.com
Website: www.unicornbooks.in • www.kidscorner.in

Distributors

Pustak Mahal, Delhi
E-mail: info@pustakmahal.com • *Website:* www.pustakmahal.com

Branches

Bengaluru, Mumbai, Patna, Hyderabad

ISBN 978-81-7806-171-9

Edition : 2009

Printed at : Param Offsetters, Okhla, New Delhi-110020

Dedication

I dedicate this book
to my parents –
Mr Amaresh Sharma
who has been a
wonderful father, and
Mrs Arati Sharma
who has been a
great mother.
Without them,
I wouldn't have the
life of satisfaction
which I have now.
They are my role
models for serving
the society. The
'service mentality'
is a gift which I
received from them
out of many other
beautiful gifts.

Preface

18th March, 2008, I was busy with my regular counselling work. Suddenly, I received a call from a gentleman. I told him about my work which I was doing for kids and the training which I give to their parents. To my surprise, he responded, "Hey, why don't you write a book on the problems which children and their parents usually face so that you are able to serve numerous kids as well as their parents?"

Though the idea was good, it vanished from my mind within a few days due to my regular work schedule. Moreover, I had always felt that book writing was the job of those people who had good command over language.

One week later, I again received a call from the same gentleman. "What about your book?" he asked. "Yes sir, I am thinking and I shall start it when I get time", I replied. He instantly motivated me that book writing is nothing if I had flow of thoughts. 'Is it so simple?' I kept pondering. 'If so, then why not, I do have flow of thoughts', I said to myself. And yes, I do wish to help kids, as many as possible.

But somehow the good idea disappeared soon.

I again got a call from the same gentleman, who said, "See, I feel you must start writing now. I shall help you. I am going to mail you the steps about writing a book. I think many parents are waiting to have relevant tips from you to take care of their children. When you have the skill, why don't you transfer your skills to the society?"

This time, he was firm. And thus, my journey started.

I wish that my journey of helping the society never ends. The way parents give me positive feedback having practised the tips and techniques which I mention in my workshops, I wish this book proves to be a turning point for numerous kids and their parents and bring about a real change in their family life. A parent simply needs to believe that he/she can do wonders to his/her child's personality and life.

I feel a separate book can be written about those people who are the backbone of this book. But, I would try to make the story short and crisp. As mentioned earlier, this book could never have been written without the support of Mr Shammi Sukh; who himself is a well-known author. His constant monitoring instilled serious discipline within me.

Going back to my childhood, I remember my parents, Mr Amaresh Sharma and Mrs Arati Sharma who always said, "This girl will do something for society." At that time, society used to be a big word for me, but I felt that they were talking about something which I need to do when I grow up. I think those statements got into my sub-conscious and this book might be a result of that positive parenting. I would like to thank them for giving me the love and support which I needed in good and bad times of my life.

My sister, Develeena, who is also a parent, keeps on asking about some or the other problem she faces with her son. Those questions stimulated my thoughts in various ways. I thank her for appreciating me in whatever I do and making me her guide of 'parenting skills'

My experience in parenting has come from handling my wonderful son – Hemang. Honestly speaking, he is my role-model. My sincere thanks to Hemang for giving me various moments of joy!

The cases presented in the book and the tips given are on the basis of the trust of several parents who had confidence in my skill, come with problems, practised the tips and given me confidence in return with their positive results. I thank all those parents for making me an expert in the field of parenting. I am confident of helping various other parents in the form of this book.

Foreword

This foreword could have been written by some famous or prominent personality. But I am neither famous nor a prominent personality. A question might be arising in your mind, i.e. how can it be that a book's foreword is being written by a common person. Yes! Because this book is for every common person.

I am sure that Nivedita's tips and suggestions can not only help kids but even change their lives as well, as it has happened in the case of my own daughter. She was a slow learner from the very beginning and had a troubled childhood. As she started growing up, her interest in studies declined further. As a matter of fact, she never passed any class without getting compartments after 6th standard and ultimately failed in 11th standard. It was then when I met Ms. Nivedita. Though initially I felt that it would be of no help even then I thought of giving it a try by giving her some counselling.

And, it was that very day and time which changed the whole life of my daughter. The change is unimaginable. I had thought of marrying her off after her passing class 12th, and you would be astonished to know that at present she is pursuing her graduation in Information and Communication in France from Soubourn University, Paris. You would be surprised to know that my daughter, Komal, who used to run away from studies during her childhood, now aspires to become an author. Today I am a happy, confident and a proud mother.

I wish I could have met Nivedita when my daughter was a small child so that she would not have lost her precious childhood. I could have been a better parent to her.

I recommend each and every parent to take full advantage from this book to give a better world to their children. This book will prove to be a real turning point for every family who follows the tips and techniques mentioned therein.

I thank Nivedita, who is now my dearest friend, who has helped me with her techniques and I wish her all the best in her mission to give children a better life by creating a turning point by empowering parents with better and practical parenting skills.

Yesterday, it was my turn of turning into a happy and proud parent. Today, it may be yours.

Satnam Kaur
A Happy Mother
paxxfashions@gmail.com

Problems & Solutions

I Hate My Books

Nine-years-old Ritwik is a high tech boy. He is interested in video games and TV, but cannot concentrate in his studies at all. His mother, Mrs Kalpana, is very unhappy with his reading and study habits. But his father, Mr Rajat, is proud of his hi-tech son. He finds his son to be highly intelligent. He enjoys the company of his son when he shows him various things on the computer. He also feels proud when his son tells him about various things he observes on T.V. But when it is time to study, it becomes a trouble for both Ritwik and his mother. He will not read a single sentence. Everyday, she struggles to manage his homework. If she complains to her husband about the problem, he simply tells her not to limit Ritwik within the boundary of school syllabus. But how can she? Being a career-oriented person, she does not want her son to lag behind in school. Moreover, she has just received a complaint from his class teacher that he has become absent-minded.

There are many children who are very intelligent. They surprise their parents as far as their intelligence in computers is concerned. But why do they not study? There are many families where parents wish to give all kinds of knowledge to their children. They bring various educational CDs for their children. Children become experts in computers. Parents too feel good when children watch educational programmes on the T.V. They feel proud with the increasing knowledge of their children.

But the children are not friendly with their books, creating problem for the parents. Mothers feel that the child cannot study without being scolded. Study time becomes a struggle time. These children try to avoid study at any cost. If parents do not take care of their studies, they lag behind in school. To see the child being responsible towards studies remains a distant dream. But parents keep on thinking about

the reason behind their lack of interest in studies and complain about their problem to the teachers. Teachers report the same thing to the parents without any solution. Gradually, the child starts hating books. He gets criticism in studies and lots of praise for his intelligence. So, he creates a balance in himself. Due to the intelligence, he gets immense appreciation from people around him. So, his self-esteem remains intact till he manages his studies with the help of his mother.

The important issue is why such intelligent children are not interested in books? Why do they lack reading skills? Is it because their eye movement does not match their understanding ability? This could be one of the reasons. It can also be that they lack concentration. But this is a reason which one might doubt. If he cannot concentrate, then, how is he able to see television for almost the whole day? Lack of concentration may be a reason, but this cannot be confirmed without any assessment. But for an intelligent child, like Ritwik, both these reasons do not apply. He was very intelligent and could learn anything through computer-aided programmes or TV programmes.

If the problem is because of lack of co-ordination between eye movement and understanding, then, a simple technique needs to be followed. The child may be instructed to read one sentence and explain the meaning of the sentence. This may create some difficulty initially, but can be very useful. This would help in improving the child's concentration as well as understanding ability. Parents can record the progress on a daily basis.

What helped Ritwik and Mrs Kalpana?

As usual, Ritwik was busy with his computer learning. His father was highly satisfied, while his mother highly dissatisfied. The father's joy lay in finding intelligence in his questions and answers while working on the computer. His mother's dissatisfaction was in finding him lagging behind in school. She did not like her intelligent son being considered below average in school.

One day, his mother was so frustrated that she stopped him from watching TV. Ritwik complained about this to his father. But there was an agreement between his mother and his father. No one would interfere in each other's disciplines. So, his father had no choice. But the disadvantage was, he drowned himself more and more in the computer. He started playing video games, and other educational games which his father brought for him. Gradually, he started developing more interest in video games than the educational games. He said that he was busy with educational games but his mother found him playing only video games.

Now, she became firm in fixing time for his computer involvement. She allowed him to be with his computer only on Sundays. This firmness was too much for him. He tried to dissuade her by crying, shouting, screaming, but Mrs. Kalpana was sure that her firmness would have a positive outcome. There was a lot of resistance from him but his mother was fully prepared with calmness to face this resistance.

Gradually, within a week, Ritwik started being with books. He started searching for story books in his shelf. But he was interested in the books which consisted more of pictures. Mrs Kalpana was happy that at least Ritwik started being with books. She also gives him company when he is with his books.

It took some time, but Ritwik overcame his problem. But why did he have this problem? How TV viewing or computer educational learning was stopping him from reading his books? The reason was when Ritwik was involved in seeing TV or computer learning, he was used to moving pictures. But when he opened his books, he found everything stationary. It seemed very dull to him. He did not find any thrill in the books. But as soon as his TV and computer involvement was restricted, his brain system was getting tuned in with the new forced system. Children can adapt to new situations better than adults. They try to find their own ways to deal with their boredom. Ritwik started being with his story books, with his craft work and his other toys which enhanced his reading skills.

Summary:

Care should be taken that children do not get addicted to learning only from moving pictures. Children, who get involved in TV or computer games, or learning through computerised educational system on a regular basis, may get addicted to them and as a result may get away from their regular study. They find it very difficult to read a single line as they want their books to be moving, colourful and full of pictures. It is better to restrict the TV and computer involvement and give exposure to various books so that the child starts enjoying reading the books. Initially, books can consist of more pictures so that the child gets friendly with the book. Later, the child would naturally search for books of his own interest. The child can be taken to an open book shop where he can search his own books. Even being a member of the library can help him/her to be with books. Whatever the case may be, it is better to restrict the TV and computer games and involve them with other games, physical activities and books.

02

I am a Duffer!

Eleven-year-old Sneha, studying in class VI, forgets whatever she learns. Her parents, Mr and Mrs Khattar, teach her and struggle hard to help her memorise everything. But within two hours she forgets ninety percent of what she has learnt. Her parents often slap and beat her. They feel that they have to beat her. They struggle hard for two to three hours to make her learn few answers, but she forgets everything. So, they find it ridiculous. How much patience can they have? After all, they are also human beings. They are more frustrated because she was very good at studies till class II. How could she deteriorate so much?

There are many children who cannot remember what they have learnt. Parents of such children become fed up with their habit of forgetting. But the point is: do they do it intentionally? Is it that they are less intelligent? Parents think so. These children are frequently called by various names like, "idiot", "duffer", etc. They are also beaten up when they forget.

It was a similar situation for Sneha too. She received no affection due to her habit of forgetting things. Moreover, she was also a victim of various other comments. Whenever she reminded her parents of any promise which they made, immediately she would get a negative reply from her mother: "Yes, except studies you can remember everything. You simply enact drama and nothing else. I don't know you are taking revenge on me for which mistake in life!" Sneha had nothing to say. She had to forget the promise. Whenever she went to sleep, lots of negative statements floated in her ears. She cursed herself for forgetting things. "Why do I forget?" She frequently asked herself but could find no answer.

Such children forget because of many reasons. One major reason might be because they find no meaning of what they are studying. They simply mug up and then vomit out what they have learnt. Children, being most creative and imaginative, see it as a punishment. They have a habit of thinking out of boundary, which the mugging up system does not allow. This creates a clash between their natural urge and the forced system. Majority of the children learn this technique due to fear of punishment. But some cannot. They become the odd child out and need to get ready for much more strict treatment.

Another reason is that children act as passive learners. Teachers or parents spend time to make the concepts clear to the child. The child does not make any effort to understand or experiment with their curiosity. As the attention span of children is very short, they go to another world while the teachers and parents are teaching them. This creates irritation in the teachers and parents. They feel that the child is dull and cannot understand in spite all their efforts.

One important factor is that children are made mostly to use their left hemisphere (grasping words, numbers, etc.) and suppress their right hemisphere (creative, imaginative part). This causes pressure on the child as he can learn better if he uses his right hemisphere more.

It is very important to know the cause of the problem so that we can deal with it. But parents are unaware of such facts. Even Sneha's parents did not have any idea of such reasons. As she was not able to cope up with her syllabus, her parents were called by the school authorities. They had to meet the Principal of the school. The class teacher who was sitting in the principal's office made a lot of complaints. At the end, the Principal suggested "I think you need to accept it that your child is a slow learner. You need to find a special school for her. She cannot cope up in our school. You see, it is not possible for a teacher to

Wonderful! Don't worry. If you can remember 2 lines, you can also say a whole paragraph.

look after one child when there are 50 children in the class! You think about it. I can help you with a few special schools which I know."

Her parents took permission for one week to come back with a decision. Sneha had a terrible day after they came back from school. Her father was not able to control himself and he thrashed her very badly. Her mother cried out of frustration. Poor Sneha could do nothing. Perhaps, she will have to live like this for her whole life!

What helped Sneha and her parents?

Just one week remained for her parents to make their decision. They visited various special schools. But Sneha was very scared. She did not want to change her school.

One evening, she was sitting in the balcony and crying alone. While she was crying, a lady was standing in the opposite balcony. This lady saw Sneha crying and could not control herself from coming to her house. The lady came to her house and shared her wish to get introduced to the family since she was new to the place. Though Mrs Khattar did not feel like smiling, she was forced to smile out of courtesy. When the lady came in she was more interested in meeting the girl who was still in the balcony. Tactfully she asked about how many members are there in the family. Mrs Khattar mentioned about her husband and her daughter. This lady now got the opportunity to ask about her daughter, expecting it would be the same girl whom she saw in the balcony. Mrs Khattar called out Sneha. But she did not reply. The lady realised the reason and she took permission from Mrs Khattar to go the balcony and found Sneha crying bitterly. The lady held her tight with affection and brought her into the room. She said, "I am Niharika. I have come to be your friend. But for that you need to smile."

It took some time to stop Sneha from crying. In between, her mother said, "Stop your drama in front of others." Niharika signalled Mrs Khattar to be quiet.

Niharika first developed a good rapport with Sneha. Then she asked Mrs Khattar about her problem. So Niharika asked Sneha to bring a book and a rough copy. Sneha felt that her image will be spoilt in front of this sweet stranger. So she tried to postpone. As Niharika was very firm she had to bring her Social Studies book, which she was most afraid of. Niharika opened the last chapter, being sure that

Sneha has not gone through that chapter even once and asked her to read one line. Then she asked her to explain what she read. But Sneha could not. Niharika said with affection, "No problem, you have read very well. I know you can explain too. It needs time. You can read it again."

Sneha was surprised to hear such sentences. "It needs time!" What is this? She had always heard, "Can't you understand such a simple sentence?" This time it was totally opposite. But she was feeling good. She read the sentence again and was able to explain. Niharika made her read an entire paragraph and asked her what she had understood in it. Sneha was able to recall 40%. Niharika seemed to be very happy. She immediately said, "I could not have recalled so well. You are so intelligent! Wonderful!" Sneha could not believe. She asked, "Are you joking Aunty?" Niharika's tone softened. She took Sneha close to her and said, "No, I mean it and I will take permission from your parents to prove it."

Mrs Khattar saw a ray of hope through Niharika. Her husband initially found it a waste of time and money. But when he came to know that Niharika is not charging anything, he was shocked. He felt there is no harm in taking this last chance. After all, he had no way out.

The only thing which Niharika did was to change Sneha from passive learner to active learner. She made Sneha explain everything. She acted as if Sneha is a teacher and she herself is the student. This gave Sneha tremendous confidence. Whenever she explained one part, Niharika praised her as one of her best teachers. Many a time, Niharika posed to be a dull student mentioning that she cannot understand until and unless Sneha explained her with diagram or points. Sneha became an expert in giving points. Moreover, Niharika asked her to make her learn the answers. She knew that Sneha will learn automatically in the process. All these were done in front of her parents. They felt guilty about how bad they treated this sweet girl. Whenever their daughter explained a point with confidence, there was a glow on parents' face. They were sure now that Sneha would succeed.

Sneha succeeded finally. They went to her school and asked them to take her test. The school authorities were sure that Sneha could not do well. They asked her to prepare only two chapters. The test would be for 25 marks. Sneha started preparing for the test with Niharika. In fact, now she started teaching Niharika. Niharika kept on giving her positive strokes of confidence. Sneha secured 22 in the paper. Her teachers and Principal were surprised.

There was no looking back for Sneha. She made a lot of new friends. Her parents accepted their mistake and said sorry to her. She was indeed full of so much affection that she forgot all the beatings and negative comments of her parents. But she always feels in her heart that no parent should spoil the self- esteem of their child. She always feels that no child should cry alone in the balcony, in the bathroom, or at night. She has dedicated her life to inject confidence in young children.

Summary:

Children might have problems of forgetting due to anxiety. Many a time, when children are constantly scolded or beaten because they forget things or they made some mistake while writing, the habit of forgetting or the mistake keeps on increasing. This happens because of the increase in their anxiety. Moreover, when children are frequently reminded that they forget, their subconscious catches such statements and stores them within. The child accepts that he/she has the problem of forgetting and nothing can be done about it. It is better to never say that the child forgets. Research says that 75% of new learning is very normal after 24 hours. But we can reduce this percentage by giving meaning to the new learning. This can be done only when the child enjoys the learning material. It is always better that the child reads and explains any new material. Parents can do the work of a facilitator. They can help the child in gaining confidence through various statements like "You learn so fast", "I am proud of your learning capacity", "I wish to learn from you how you explain so well", etc. All these would create a positive learning graph. Moreover, rather than focusing on marks, parents need to focus on understanding the concepts. When parents make results a status issue, it creates pressure on the child. When the result is out or some paper is given, first see what is there to appreciate. Do find some. Then see what needs to be done for improvement. Parents should never blame and curse the child for their mistake, they should know what improvement needs to be done and then sit and plan some strategy for improvement. Stick to the strategy on a regular basis. Do not try to be a parent only when the result is declared. Be a parent throughout.

I Can Never Be Fast !

Bahaar studies in class VI. She is an average and a quiet student. She is very attached to her mother. Bahaar's mother, Vibha, handles her daughter very well. She rarely raises her voice to control her. In fact, Bahaar is so wonderful that it is not required to raise one's voice to control her. But as every parent has complains, same was with Vibha. According to her, Bahaar is average in academics but she is slow in every other thing. Her father scolds her all the time with the hope that she would do better. Once a week, her father takes a class of two hours for Bahaar. Being a quiet child, she just listens without any clarification. But next day she is at her own pace. These days, she has also become absent-minded.

There are many parents like Vibha who face such problem with their children. They complain about their child being slow. "Quick", "hurry", "fast", "rush", etc., are the frequently used words in such families. The child feels confused because they do not understand the parents' expectations. According to them, they are doing as fast as they can. Many children feel frustrated and start arguing. Children like Bahaar suffer internally.

At the foremost, it is required to know what can be the disadvantages of the way such children are handled. These children receive end number of lectures, scolding and sometimes even beaten. Some parents opine that after the children are beaten or scolded, they listen for some time, but again goes back to their regular pace. They feel that if the children can increase their pace through scolding or beating, why can't they make it a habit? All such questions remain unanswered.

Everybody agreed that Bahaar was slow. But they also agreed that Bahaar had a lot of qualities. She was very creative. She used to take care of her younger sister like a mother. The way she took care of her mother's emotions touched everyone's heart. She was always ready to give her things to anyone. She would never eat anything alone. If something is given to her, she would keep it for her mother, father and sister.

But these days, Bahaar had become absent-minded. This problem worried her parents. She falls down all of a sudden while walking on the road; she brings water and it falls. The nervousness and anxiety has started showing on her face. She does not want such things to happen to her but she is helpless. She feels all these things happen automatically. The more she takes care to be careful, the more she proves herself to be careless. So, now her mother has stopped her from carrying any breakable utensils.

Bahaar feels sad and cries many a times. She wants to change herself and prove that she can do things fast. But whenever she tries, she proves the opposite. She has started accepting that she might be abnormal as her father says. Many a time, her mother consoles her and tries to make her understand with soft words. She cries holding her mother without saying a single word. She says internally, "Mamma, believe me. I do not do it intentionally. I want to be fast. I don't want to be scolded. I feel bad when you beat me. I don't want to break the glass. I want to help you. I love you." All these sentences remain in Bahaar's heart. But she is never able to say a single sentence. Only her tears flow.

If such scene continues, Bahaar would not only remain slow and absent-minded, but along with these two other negative and problematic behaviours would also emerge. Vibha was scared. As Bahaar was so sensitive, she wanted her to be bold, fast and spontaneous so that she can face life in a better way. But Vibha found no way out to fulfil her wish.

What helped Bahaar and her parents?

One day, Bahaar and her friend, Vidushi, were sitting in the school reception and waiting for their parents. Vidushi's mother arrived early. Vidushi's mother started talking to Bahaar and her own daughter. Vidushi's mother liked the calm and composed nature of Bahaar and appreciated Bahaar as she was speaking very softly. But Bahaar was unable to take the appreciation and said, "But aunty, I am very slow."

FINISH LINE

This sentence touched Vidhushi's mother. She was able to sense the pain. Immediately she said, "Yes, it may be. I would say, you do things so carefully that you make less mistakes." Bahaar recalled her mistake and said, "But aunty, I have broken a new glass at home. I have dropped water twice while I was carrying it for guests." Vidushi's mother felt like sitting with Bahaar for a long time. She said, "Bahaar, do you give water to guests? That sounds wonderful. You know I think you can teach many children of your age to be as good as you are."

By that time, Vibha had arrived. Vidushi's mother felt very nice to see both mother and daughter hugging each other. There was reflection of true affection in their gesture. Vibha moved forward and hugged Vidushi which gave a feeling of joy to Vidushi's mother. But Vidushi's mother was anxious to talk to Vibha. She took her number and departed.

Vidushi's mother reached Vibha's place in the weekend. She shared with Vibha the conversation which she had had with Bahaar. Vibha started sharing her own pain. She told her about the pain they need to undergo to make Bahaar drink milk in the morning. Vidushi's mother listened to Vibha's complaints and said, "Vibha, you want to give her milk for her physical development but the words both you and your husband use during that time is ruining her mental and emotional development. Will you let it happen? You want her to be fast in several tasks, but she is becoming low in her self-confidence. Do you want her to be a fast machine at the cost of her self-esteem? Will you let all her positive feelings and emotions die? What would the 'fast-ness' do if the child within her dies? Your child is becoming too anxious. Try to deal with her anxiety more than her pace."

"But how?" this was the question pondering in Vibha's mind. She was moved by the words of Vidushi's mother. She felt guilty of her actions. How could she not understand what a stranger came and identified? But she was thankful to God that at least she was shown the other side of the coin. She reviewed that 80% of Bahaar's waking time was spent in trying to make her increase her speed. Vibha discussed with her husband. He, too, realised his mistake, but he was also confused about what to do.

Now the experimentation time started for both Vibha and her husband. Before going to sleep at night, Vibha asked Bahaar what she would like to eat in the morning. Bahaar immediately replied, "Mamma, is there an option tomorrow?" Vibha nodded her head with a smile. Bahaar thought for a while. She asked, "Can I eat one small parantha with curd? Is it possible that I don't drink milk in morning?" Vibha again nodded. Next day, it was slightly easy for Bahaar. She was fond of curd. So eating parantha with curd was not very difficult. But Vibha had to interfere in between to increase her speed. But this time, she just smiled and mentioned that she wants Bahaar to eat a bite from her hand. Bahaar was really happy. Vibha noted the time taken by Bahaar in every activity that day. She appreciated her to do most of the work by herself.

Next day, Vibha made her wake up 15 minutes before her actual waking time. She did this to give more comfort to Bahaar. This made the morning easier for Bahaar. Vibha and her husband appreciated Bahaar to have done all her work by herself. They accepted that Bahaar had her own pace but due to her pace, they would not spoil her confidence. They started changing the schedule in such a way that Bahaar could do all her work with ease. Vibha added tact in between. She made the milk time just before her play time. As Bahaar wanted to play with her friends, she tried to manage drinking milk faster than her regular pace. Her motivation level to finish the milk was high at this time.

Her parents stopped using the word absent-minded. They started saying, "Bahaar, you observe things so well." There were times when Bahaar fell while walking, but they just helped her in getting up and said, "it's O.K. Get up you brave girl!" Gradually, Bahaar was more focused while walking on road. She herself also did not want to fall. But the words "It's O.K." seemed to be a great support. They were sure that they would not use such words that would multiply the problems. They kept on thinking about many ways to formulate the words in such a way that could increase Bahaar's confidence level. She being a sensitive girl, those powerful words worked like magic. At least, she did not feel low due to her slow pace. She felt comfortable with herself. She felt that she is loved by her parents. She realised that now she does not give pain to her parents. This realisation gave great relief to Bahaar.

Summary:

Children who are slow have a secondary problem of losing their self-esteem. They are criticised so much for being slow that they tend to withdraw from many activities. They feel that they would be a failure. The sense of failure acts as a slow poison. This slow poison increases many other unpredictable problems. The best way to deal with this slow pace is "motivation". The motivation needs to be positive. The child needs to be encouraged and appreciated for all the work he/she is doing by himself or herself. Moreover, the tasks where the child finds lots of difficulties need to be rescheduled in such a manner that the child does not feel any pain in doing them. It is better to remove the word "slow" from the dictionary and instead observe the tasks which the child does well. Then it may be said, "You did these works so well." This would enhance the self-esteem of the child. Every one has strengths and weaknesses. Parents need to focus on the positive ones so that they keep on increasing.

Just 5 minutes!

Just Five Minutes Mamma!

Ronit never completes his work on time. He has developed the habit of postponing every activity, be it studies, taking bath or eating food. His five minutes never end. Mrs Kataria, Ronit's mother, is worried with his habit. She has to scream to make Ronit do anything. She starts sweetly but ends up with a harsh voice. She starts saying from the kitchen, "Ronit, switch off the TV." But he immediately answers back, "five minutes, mamma." She comes back after half an hour and finds Ronit still viewing T.V. Now she loses her patience and tells that she has to shout. Ronit does not listen! Why does he act like this? Why he spoils his and his mother's mood? If his mother tells him to go and take bath, he will keep on sitting and again says "five minutes, mamma." If he is told to clean his almirah, immediately he will say, "five minutes mamma." When his mother wakes him up from sleep, Ronit's five minutes are still there. After he comes back from school, his mother has to scream for each work, be it for changing his dress, washing his face, or keeping the bag at its place. For each work, he would say, "I will do mamma. Just five minutes, mamma." Will his five minutes ever end?

This is a very common scene in most families. Mothers shouting and screaming is a usual phenomenon. Mothers say that they 'have to'. But do they really 'have to'? No. Actually screaming is a short-cut which parents have learnt to deal with their children. But this screaming causes more damage than good. The children who can very well read the parents' minds come to know his boundary. They know how they can extend their boundary from five minutes to two hours or may be more than that. Now very small kids of nursery have learnt to use this "five minutes" policy. They don't know what five minutes mean but use it 50 times a day.

The reason behind this postponement can be many. The major reason might be that children find regular tasks to be monotonous. They find no interest in the same things. Thinking about those works does not give them any enthusiasm. They want to avoid them. But they know that it is not possible to avoid those tasks completely. So, they find postponement as the best way to deal with this situation. They do not learn to take responsibility for those tasks. They are given punishment in terms of scolding or screaming but no strategy is used to develop their feeling of responsibility. These children like to do what interests them but do not see the long-term disadvantage in not performing certain tasks. They want to be engrossed in what they find interesting at the given moment. Children are the ones who know to live in each moment. Due to this, they do not feel the necessity of doing the tasks which do not give them a moment's feeling. Many children have learnt that mothers would shout in spite of anything. They found through their insight that mothers do find some or the other reason for screaming and shouting. So, they find no use in troubling in doing the tasks which pleases their mothers. They learnt that even if they tried many a time to please their parents, still they get scolding or harsh treatment. The good behaviour which they have demonstrated consciously had no meaning before their parents' eyes. So, there was no use making any conscious effort!

Parents need to understand that their children understand even what is unspoken. They can go beyond the words and understand the meaning of any gesture or any behaviour. Ronit had learnt that although his mother tells him to do some work, she does not mean so. This he learnt through his own observation. Initially when Ronit's mother said, "Ronit, bring your copy", Ronit replied, "Yes mamma, just bringing within five minutes." After giving this reply, Ronit managed to be with other games for another 20 minutes. Again his mother says, "Ronit, I have been telling since long to bring your copy." Ronit still tries his own strategy, "Yes mamma, just five minutes." After half an hour, his mother comes back and loses her patience. She shouts now. But Ronit found that he managed with 50 minutes. So, he thinks that five minutes is really very useful. Children may or may not be able to estimate the duration of time, but they find magic in five minutes.

Sadly parents, due to their own shortcomings, shout at their children. They do not remain firm at the first go. They train children with one method non-verbally and create confusion by verbally training them with another method.

What helped Ronit and his mother?

Ronit was used to living in this manner. But internally he used to feel disturbed when his mother screamed. He mentioned to one of his uncle that his heart beats fast when her mother shouts. Many a time, he asked his mother, "Mamma, can't you speak politely?" She gives him several explanations which he cannot understand. He simply that when his mother tells him to speak politely, why can't she?

Days were passing by in this manner. One day Mrs Kataria went to office where she shared her problem with one colleague. Her friend kept on asking questions about her daily routine. Mrs Kataria realised that she gets extremely tired after she reaches home and she cannot be patient with her son. She realised that her son's habit of postponement can be due to her own faulty behaviour. She does not remain firm initially. She instructs and goes away. She gets involved with her own work. But when she comes back and finds Ronit not over with the work, it irritates her. Her irritation needs a vent out. So, screaming comes as the best solution for her. This habit of shouting is also spoiling her relation with her son. Her friend suggested that she should ask Ronit to finish a work and report to her what all he has completed! Maybe this would develop a sense of responsibility within the child.

It has been found that there is a solution to every problem. We need to tune our mind to the solution. Mrs Kataria's mind is now tuned in towards solution. Many other things floated in her mind. She was sure that she would succeed in her mission to make her son responsible. Will Mrs Kataria's mission be successful? It's not an easy job. Mrs Kataria had lots of hopes. She just took a seat on the sofa to relax herself. Ronit came slowly with a glass of water for his mamma. This is Ronit's daily job for which he is never appreciated. But the day he misses this work, his parents never miss to comment on Ronit's lack of concern towards them. This time Mrs Kataria was feeling a lot of affection towards Ronit. She took her son close to her and hugged him. Ronit felt very cozy in his mother's arm. Mrs Kataria thanked

Ronit for the glass of water. She said, "It makes me feel so good when you give me a glass of water whenever I come from outside." Ronit looked towards his mother. His looks indicated as if he wants to check whether it is his same mother.

Now Mrs Kataria stopped listing out what Ronit needed to do. She said very calmly, "Ronit, let me see how much work you finish and by when. You complete one task and let me know about what you have done." Ronit was surprised. He asked, "But what do I need to do?" Mrs Kataria calmly replied, "Ronit, I know you are very intelligent and you know your own work." Ronit thought for a while and said, "O.K." Ronit went to his study room. Within 20 minutes he came to his mother and said, "Mamma, I have finished my homework, see." Ronit handed over his maths copy to his mother. It was a shock to Mrs Kataria. She hugged Ronit and shared her happiness. Ronit was excited today. He rushed to his room and kept on reporting about his various works: polishing his shoes, keeping his uniform ready, packing his bag for next day. It was very surprising for Ronit's mother. She only had to say, "Ronit, one work is still left!" Although she meant filling up the bottle, Ronit listed out four works for himself. Mrs Kataria felt relieved as she did not have to give stress on her memory. She felt like screaming out due to her well-formed habit. But she controlled herself. She strictly followed the new way. She even gave a reward by playing with Ronit. Ronit loved to play chess which she did frequently as a token of appreciation.

She followed this for one month consciously and it became her habit. Now, Ronit knows what he has to do. If sometimes, Ronit tried to throw his own strategy, very patiently Mrs Kataria tells, "I don't have any problem. You need to do some extra work." Ronit hated this punishment. It was easier for him to hear his mother screaming. But he knows that his mother means what she tells now. He knows that his mother has become both positive and firm. Although many times, he does not like this firmness; still he loves her positive behaviour. Ronit learnt what he cannot avoid. He also learnt that postponement brings many additional works. So, he even learnt to finish his work on time.

To develop this habit of Ronit, Mrs Kataria had to switch off the gas and stand in front of Ronit to make sure that he does not avoid. Whenever Ronit mentions about his '5 minutes', Mrs Kataria reminds him of 5 additional works. Mrs. Kataria did all these slowly and steadily so that it did not create any pressure on Ronit.

Now, Ronit is more responsible. Even when he went to his grandparents' home during summer vacation, all were able to see the difference in him. This was a great appreciation for both Ronit and Mrs Kataria.

Summary:

Postponement is a common behaviour in many children. Parents need to check whether they also practise the same behaviour pattern. If mother or father uses the word '5 minutes' and manages to escape a work for sometime, the child also learns the same. Children learn fast by observing their parents. If the parents show enjoyment in the work they do and then, shares the sense of achievement in accomplishing these regular works, the child would also learn to feel the same sense of achievement from his regular work. Parents need to give strokes of appreciation now and then, maybe by saying, "Is it? Great! You did your work so fast!" This gives meaning to the regular tasks. Rather than screaming or shouting, it is better to stand in front of the child and say with a firm voice, "I am waiting for you to get up and do your work." When he/she continues doing the work, appreciate the progress. Do not wait for the final work to give appreciation. Motivation is required in between the tasks. Parents might say, "I am feeling good that you have started your work." These things would help the child to learn to do his/her work without tendency to avoid things. If he/she does any work without anyone telling him to do so, it is always required to appreciate, maybe by saying, "Wow! It's so nice that you did your work on your own. You have such wonderful memory." But parents should not crib if children do not remember. Just give them a clue or ask them about the tasks they need to do. Parents would be surprised by their memory. Children know all they need to do. Just that screaming gave them a chance to avoid. Once parents stop screaming, children learn new and positive ways soon. Children are fast to unlearn and then to re-learn in a new way.

I am getting bored.

I am Getting Bored

Nishant's favourite dialogue is "I am getting bored." Mrs Kohli, Nishant's mother, herself has started getting bored with this statement. Why does a child of 8 years constantly get bored? Is this a psychological problem? Is it normal? Even if it is normal, it is so irritating. How can one mention the list of things a child can do if he/she is getting bored? Mrs Kohli used to mention many activities like, "Go and finish your drawing work", "OK, go and take care of your rack", etc. But with every statement he would say, "I am not feeling like doing this. If asked what he really wants to do, he would just say in his simple words, "I don't know, you say." This was a simple sentence for Nishant, but a difficult one for his mother. She could find no solution. Even when she tells him to watch T.V., he would say the same thing, "I am getting bored."

There are many houses where students use this statement of getting bored. This becomes very irritating for those handling the child. These children cannot stick to one activity for a long time. Parents might feel relieved for some time but immediately, thereafter, they will come and express their feeling of getting bored. There are many children who, when they go to anyone's place, irritates their parents by the same dialogue of getting bored. This not only creates problem for parents but also for the host where they visited.

There may be various reasons for such behaviour patterns:

1. Maybe such children are not satisfied internally. If one is not satisfied internally, no task would create any meaning. Without knowing the reason, parents work at superficial level. They try to give a list of activities in which they can engage themselves in. But it is important to work at a deeper level.

2. It may also be that there is a monotonous and dull environment in the family. Thus, children feel suffocated and no activity gives them any fun element. Parents are involved in their regular mechanical activities. They cannot understand what the need of an enthusiastic home environment is. Due to this reason, children express an their feelings by stating the activities to be boring. In fact, parents need to work on the home environment more than the activities.

3. This may also be a sign of attention-seeking behaviour. If children do not get constructive attention, they irritate parents to seek attention at any cost. Such behaviour may occur with single child or even where there are two or more siblings. Different children have different levels of hunger for attention seeking. So, it cannot be assured that if the elder child is not having this problem, younger one will also not have such problem. Or it may be vice-versa. When the younger child is born and the parent has to give more time to the second one, elder one may feel neglected.

What helped Nishant and his mother?

Nishant used to be scolded regularly after he used to nag with the same sentence. Mrs Kohli tried to be patient but had to scold him at the end. She wanted solutions for her problems.

One day she sat and analysed her behaviour. She found that many a time she also utters the statement of work being boring. She realised that Nishant must have learnt the behaviour from her. So, she decided to stop discussing about work being boring for her. She might have used it once a week and Nishant found it so useful that he uses it hundred times a day.

Next day when she got up, she shared with her son that she is finding the day to be very interesting. She shared all the work she is needed to do today which would give her a feeling of joy. She even mentioned about washing clothes and cooking as interesting. Nishant did not want to be left behind. He too mentioned that he would be completing his homework and some cutting and pasting work which he finds very interesting. She did a continuous follow-up by asking "What aspect of this work do you find interesting Nishant?" She started giving him points in sharing the positive feeling towards the work. Nishant wanted to secure more points compared to his mother. Even she wanted the same. The most interesting thing occurred when Nishant came to the kitchen and asked Mrs Kohli, "Mamma, what aspect of this cleaning work is giving you joy?" Mrs Kohli was tired doing the cleaning work. She wanted to complete the work fast and sit under the fan. Listening to her son's question, she recalled the experiment she has started. Immediately she brought a smile on her face and said, "See, I am cleaning so well. Moreover, see, I am smiling. That itself shows that I am finding the work joyful." Nishant caught the word 'smile'. Whenever any of the family members did any work with seriousness on the face, he immediately pointed out, "Are you not interested in the work?" When asked how he feels so, he used to smile. This experiment proved effective in various ways: first, Nishant started focusing on the positive aspect of any activity. Second, when he mentioned about the positive part of the activity, he got appreciation which fulfilled his attention-seeking hunger in a constructive way. Third, 'smile' changed the dull family environment into a positive environment.

But it happened that on many occassions Nishant, out of his previous habit, repeated the sentence of feeling bored. But Mrs Kohli or other members immediately reminded him of points. This compelled Nishant to find at least one positive aspect. It took approximately 15 days to make it a practice. But at the end, Mrs Kohli's experiment turned out to be effective. It happens that when we experiment with one solution, several other solutions come up automatically. It was as if that the word "boring" was banned in the family. But no one had actually banned the word, it happened by merely changing the focus.

Nishant's parents also thought that they should spend some time playing with their child. They themselves started asking Nishant, "Nishant, would you like playing badminton with us?" Nishant started feeling important. Sometimes his mother tells him, "I feel like playing chess with you. Will you give me time after we both finish our work?" Nishant happily used to say 'yes'. But one day Mrs Kohli fell in trouble. When Mrs Kohli asked Nishant to give time after completing their work, very tactfully Nishant said, "I would not mind even now. Come, let's play. We can complete our work later." Mrs Kohli was in a dilemma but she managed to find a suitable sentence and said, "Nishant, I would feel more comfortable when we both complete our work." Nishant tried to get his own way politely but Mrs Kohli was firm. She even mentioned that she won't be able to play at all if they stuck in this argument of when to play. Nishant thought it was wise to be quiet than to continue with his convincing ability.

Children learn fast but we need to tune our mind to solutions. Once we know the exact reason behind the problem, it becomes easy to find steps for modification.

Summary:

There are many children who may use the sentence, "I am feeling bored. What should I do?" Rather than focusing on the sentence at the surface level, it is important to find the reason which may be hidden at a deeper level. The child may be internally upset with various things. It is important that parents do talk to the child. Children can even be asked to tell stories. Parents would know the need of the child through the story. But parents need to instruct the child to tell original stories created by him. They can play it as a game. Parents need to give constructive appreciation to the child. Moreover, parents need to check the environment of the home and make it creative and constructive. If the parents dance or play with the child, it can create a good bond between the parents and child. This bond will give a sense of security. The point technique has also been very useful in such cases. Children feel great when they secure points for their positive work. Parents can take help of this need and the child will also fulfil his/her appreciation hunger. Parents can also think about various other techniques once they find the reason of the problem. The benefits of these techniques are that they do not have any side effects.

I don't Want to Go to School

Each morning it is a struggling time at Kanishk's home. Will Kanishk go to school today? If yes, how? His mother starts waking up this seven-year-old child who has started throwing tantrums since one month. "I will not go to school", "Promise, I will go tomorrow", "Not today... please papa", "Mamma, I miss you in the school", etc. Sometimes he is sent to school by scolding him, sometimes he has to be bribed with the promise of a chocolate or ice-cream. Sometimes, his parents have to give in to his stubbornness. After staying back at home, Kanishk had a gala time watching TV and playing computer games with the repeated conditions flowing from parents that he has to go to school the next day. Only under this condition he has the privilege to watch TV or enjoy computer games. But all such conditions fail as soon as the next morning comes.

This is a common scene in many families. This may occur at any stage, of course, the reasons vary. Kanishk developed this 'school phobia' after completing two years of proper schooling experience. This was indeed surprising for his parents. They went to his school and discussed with his teachers. The teachers started pampering him a lot. Kanishk was aware of what was happening. He started taking advantage of the situation. He stopped doing all his work stating that he wants to go home as he is not feeling well. After every class, he had to be sent to the medical room, from the medical room he is sent back to his class because he had no problem. His teachers and family struggled to make him comfortable in the school but in vain. His parents provided him with every privilege hoping for better response the next day. The teachers stopped pressurising him to complete his homework hoping that this would motivate him to come to school.

Please, I won't go to school today.
Ok, but you have to study continuously and I mean it.

But gradually his friends rejected him. He was not able to answer the questions asked in the class which de-motivated him more. He lost interest in his studies, school, friends and teachers. Everybody could now associate only one sentence with Kanishk – I want to go home. Nobody could find out where the problem was. They could not figure out why Kanishk was behaving in this way.

What helped Kanishk and his parents?

Kanishk's parents were pondering on how to find out a solution to Kanishk's problem. One day, a family friend came to visit them. He came to know about Kanishk's problem and enquired how they were dealing with it. Kanishk's parents mentioned that they are fulfilling each and every demand of Kanishk hoping for a better morning. They showed the toy rack of Kanishk which was filled with new and expensive toys. Nothing seemed to work for Kanishk. He enjoys everything till the evening, promising that he will not create any problem the next morning. But he forgets everything when the time comes.

They discussed his daily schedule and ultimately found out a solution. It took just one more day to handle the problem.

Kanishk is now in class VII. His parents are relaxed and happy. He enjoys his school and his studies as much as he enjoys his friends' company. But what helped Kanishk all of a sudden? Let us analyse.

Kanishk had developed this problem after his summer vacation. For two months he got used to living his life in his own way. This became his habit. When his school re-opened after summer vacation, he was not comfortable with the change in his routine. Whenever Kanishk managed to stay at home, he had the opportunity to go back to his comfort zone of enjoyment.

Even if he had to go to school, he managed to have all sorts of enjoyment when he returned from school.

In the school too, his teachers sympathised and pampered him. Neither did he have to study nor did he get any scolding for his homework. After his parents discussed about his problem with their family friend, they got to know the root cause of the problem. They found that Kanishk is enjoying the routine he is following at home while other students are struggling to complete their homework, learn new lesson. So, they tried a method.

One day when Kanishk said that he would not go to school, they said that they are fine with the idea. Kanishk was shocked. But they were firm that he has to get up even if he does not want to go to school. Kanishk had to give in to this demand to escape from school. After finishing all his work, his mother instructed that he has to put on his school dress and be on the study table by 8 a.m. (school time). The new rule was explained to him. First, he would only have the half an hour break as given in school. Second, he would study as per school time table till 2 p.m. When he enquired about games period his mother told him the third rule, no games period on the day he does not go to school. Kanishk thought that he would be allowed to watch TV after 2.00 p.m. His mother told him the fourth rule about no TV, no computer games, and no visits to the park on the day he does not go to school.

Kanishk threw all his tantrums in order to have his demands fulfilled. But his parents were firm. Next day Kanishk, due to his habit, said that he will not go to school but he recalled everything. He realised that it is better to go to school and to have games and other activity periods along with other enjoyments with friends than to have monotonous study time at home.

Summary:

To deal with any kind of school phobia at any stage, first try to find out the root cause. Take the first step of talking to the teachers. Check what you can do at home. Rather than fulfilling the child's demands, stop rewarding him for negative behaviour pattern. Keep on appreciating his positive behaviour. Talk to the child to know the real reason and avoid giving pressure on him/her by asking too many questions. Follow an effective lifestyle in the family. Ensure that the child gets proper sleep. Avoid TV or computer games just before sleep. This might make the child anxious. Relaxing stories will help in making the child wake up fresh the next morning. Keep friendly behaviour at home. Make a daily routine for the child, including both studies and leisure.

07

I am so Hungry!

Mrs Sheetal feels shy to take her son Yash to any place. Wherever he goes, he complains about his hunger. She feeds him properly before going out. But still, he asks for biscuits, mixture or anything he sees. Once he went to someone's place and demanded one biscuit. He was provided with one biscuit. Then, he asked for another. He was provided with two more. He finished the two and said, "Why don't you give me the whole packet?" This was too much. Everyone feels how this three-year-old child who cannot even speak properly can eat so much! But he did. He avoided rice and chapatti but he could compete with any adult member as far as biscuits or namkeen was concerned.

There are many children who like to eat biscuits, mixtures, or any other fast food. But if it is too much, it is a cause of concern. Yash sounds very irritating when he goes to anyone's place. His mother is more concerned as she feels very embarrassed. She scolds him and stops him from asking for anything. But he can never control himself. After all, how could he eat so much? His mother tried to give all the food of his choice. But his problem did not reduce even a little.

Yash's mother was working on dealing with physiological hunger. She was not able to realise that his hunger was not physiological in nature, but it was emotional hunger. Yash was a single child. His parents had taken divorce when he was just 11months old. He was taken care of by the maid till he was two years old. Thereafter, he used to stay in a crèche. His mother was serving in an organisation and her office hours were from 9 a.m. to 5 p.m. After reaching home, she used to be so tired that she had no time for her son. She used to slap him for every mistake of his. When Yash wanted to play with his mother, she wanted him to eat fast and go to sleep so that she can prepare herself for the next day's tasks.

Parents' divorce usually becomes a curse for children. The single parent needs to be more cautious about the emotional development of the child. When the child observes other children moving with both parents or talking about both parents, they feel this absence more. This creates an emotional pain which they cannot express verbally. It comes out through behaviour symptoms. With Yash, this behaviour symptom was overeating at others' place.

Some children might go into their shell and withdraw from any social interaction. Others may become very aggressive. Others may cling on to certain relations and would try to compensate the absence of any one parent by being close with someone in whom he/she can mentally see the figure of the absent parent. If the person whom he/she relates to does not fulfil his emotional hunger, he might tend to be internally upset. While all these problems go on in the child's mind, no one can understand the real problem from his external behaviour.

Mrs Sheetal needs help so that she can handle Yash better. She needs to see beyond the external behaviour of Yash. How can Sheetal do so? She is extremely busy earning money for her and her son's living. Will Yash be a permanent victim of hunger? Will his hunger ever end?

What helped Yash and his mother?

Life went on with irritation and aggression in both Yash and his mother. Yash used to feel very comfortable in any adult male company. More than spending time with any friend of his own age group, he loved to sit on the lap of any of his uncles. Whenever any male used to come to his place, he tried to be with him to the maximum time. This used to irritate Sheetal.

Days were passing like this. There was an acquaintance who used to visit Yash's family. He was friendly with Yash. They used to play together, study together and enjoy each other's company. Sheetal used to feel very good to see both of them playing. This person made Sheetal understand that Yash is looking for a father figure. He mentioned that Sheetal needs to be more loving and understanding towards Yash. Sheetal gave it a thought and found what he said to be sensible. She started spending more time with Yash. She started playing with him which she never did earlier. She started listening to his strange questions. In fact, she started enjoying these questions and his lovely answers.

One day, Yash, his mother and the acquaintance were sitting together. Yash shared his wish, "Why don't you both marry?" The acquaintance, being very understanding, asked him why he wants his mother and him to marry. Yash said with soft voice, "So that you stay with me forever. In every family there is a father. I also want to say others that my father stays with me." The acquaintance said, "But I take you to Children's Park, I play with you, I love you so much!" Yash gave a straight answer, "But you can only become a father if you marry my mamma."

A child knows everything. He has all the information. Yash's mother was very surprised to hear the dialogue between both of them. How could a small child speak such stuff?

Sometimes we are so occupied with our own stress, with our self-created tensions that we do not look into the stress of our children. Yash was also a victim of stress. When his friends used to talk about their fathers, about how they wait for their fathers, he used to feel the vacant space in his heart. Can he never get his father? He started going to the temple with the hope that some day God will send him a father. He shared this with his mother one day.

I am feeling very upset as I don't have a father.
Yes, I do understand and I also know that you are a brave boy to handle this feeling. I am with you dear.
P. Gaul

She was touched and deeply wanted to fulfil his wish. But she knew that being a divorced woman and having a child was a great disadvantage for a person's marriage in India. She also had the fear of taking a second chance. She was surrounded with too many "What if...." statements. At the end she decided that she would take care of her son herself and give him most of her quality time. Although she cannot wipe out Yash's desire to have a father figure, but at least she can do her own part.

As Sheetal started focusing on her own behaviour and giving more and more time to Yash, the same person, whom Yash admired and whom he wanted to be his father, shared his desire to marry Sheetal. She was quite confused. But looking at the bond between him and her son, she felt she should take the decision. They got married and when Yash for the first time called this person Papa, there was a lot of happiness in his eyes.

Yash started believing more in God. His father loves him a lot. He changed Sheetal's belief of creating a perfect child and made her understand and accept Yash as a child. Sheetal started showering her love and affection on both her husband and her son. Theirs became the ideal family.

There would be many single parents who may not be as fortunate as Sheetal. Still, they can do their own share of showering love and affection on their children. It is important to listen to them. Let them vent out their internal feelings. Parents need to keep the door of sharing open. If the feelings are stored inside, it creates more damage. If the child shares the desires and emotions, it acts as a healing element.

It is better to be an emotional healer than being merely a problem solver for the child. If parents act as emotional healers, then the child can be a wonderful problem solver too.

Summary:

In today's world, single parenting is a complex issue. During the moment of decision making for a divorce, everything seems to be very manageable. In fact, both the parents only think about how they are going to manage. No one thinks about how the children are going to manage. It would be better if parents do not take divorce thinking about their children. Second task would be to work on the relationship so that the bitter relation turns better. But if divorce is the ultimate solution, the parent taking care of the child needs to be emotionally mature. He/she needs to spend sufficient time with the child. The child will grow with 'the time' he gets, and not with 'the money' the parent earns. It is better to give the child maximum time rather than maximum facilities. A ten-rupees toy would be as much valuable for him as one of thousand rupees. In the given time, talking and sharing of feelings is very important. The parent may give various positive strokes during that shared time. They can be through various statements like, "I feel proud of you the way you manage your own work", "I get so much strength through you", "You are the best gift I have ever got in life", "We are such good friends", etc. Such statements need to be shared with genuineness and concern. A child is intelligent enough to understand the artificiality. Let not adults' decision be the cause of pain for children. Let us not fill a child's life with stress. Let each child be a happy child.

I am so Scared

Lakshit is 10-years-old. He is scared of everything. He shivers when someone says anything in a high pitch. He is fearful of many things. He is scared to go to a room alone or to go and play outside. This has become a cause of real concern for his parents. Every time, when they try to build up courage in him, he keeps on saying, "I am feeling scared." When his parents ask him, "What you are feeling scared of?" he replies, "I don't know." Lakshit himself wants to come out of it. He mentions that in the class when teacher scolds anybody else, he shivers even then.

Many children face this problem of "fear". A number of times it can be related to a past experience, but sometimes it is just a creation of their imagination. If something fearful had occurred in the past, the child keeps on using his imaginative skills to remember the incident again and again, especially when the child does not get a highly enthusiastic and positive environment around him.

Sometimes this fear can be a cause of some unrelated problem. If the child is not able to express his feeling of aggression or frustration in a constructive way and is made to suppress all his feelings, a lack of self-esteem occurs, which may lead to such a problem of fear.

Sometimes parents do not understand the difference between discipline and punishment causing problem in the positive development of the child. If in the initial years, a child has to undergo unhealthy parenting style, such a problem may occur.

Moreover, if both father and mother quarrel with each other, the child starts feeling insecure and this insecurity may lead to some kinds of problems. The child wants both the parents. It gives immense security to the child when he/she finds that his/her parents are attached to each other. If there is any sort of blame game, cursing or rebuking going on in the family, the child gets anxious and this anxiety may lead to secondary problems of fear.

So, we need to focus on various disciplinary patterns and their various effects on the child's future development:

☛ An authoritarian or extremely strict parent controls a child's behaviour and attitude by stressing obedience to authority and discouraging discussion. Extremely strict parents often rely on punishment. Research suggests that children raised by authoritarian strict parents tend to be timid and withdrawn, less intellectually curious and dependent on the voice of authority. They might feel fearful to take any decision in life.

☛ A moderately authoritative parent sets limits and relies on natural and logical consequences for children to learn from making their own mistakes. The parent explains why rules are important and why they must be followed. Such parents reason with their children and consider the children's point of view as well; though they might not agree with them. They are firm, but show kindness, warmth and love. They set high standards and encourage their children to be independent. They might say, "I am not feeling good about your jumping on the cushions". Their voice is not harsh but it is firm. When the child comes back to the rule, they give appreciation. They discuss a lot with their children. Children raised by moderate parents tend to be responsible, co-operative, self-reliant and intellectually curious. Such children feel safe and secure. They want to know new things. They are not afraid of committing mistakes, rather, they learn from these mistakes. They have the courage to experiment and then learn. They tend to be self-motivated.

- A permissive or indulgent parent exerts minimal control. Children are allowed to set their own rules and schedules and activities. Permissive parents do not demand the high levels of behaviour as authoritarian and authoritative parents. Children raised by permissive parents tend to be immature, reluctant to accept any responsibility or to show independence. They are habituated to do what they want. They have been given permission for anything they wanted. So, they did not learn how to postpone their demands and behaviour.

There might be other problems related to the problem of fear. It needs to be first analysed whether the fear is rational or irrational. If it is rational, simple dialogues may help. Then monitoring can be done in a positive manner. The parents or other people involved may inject confidence in the child. If the fear is irrational, help can be taken from a psychologist. If the child is scared of cockroaches or lizards or darkness or water to an excess level, a psychologist can help through various techniques called systematic desensitisation or cognitive therapy. Fear does not let us bring out our real potential. This may create problems in later life. So, it needs to be dealt with. The earlier we make an effort, the better it is.

What helped Lakshit and his parents?

Lakshit seemed to be a very obedient child. He listened to everything what was said to him. He never tells 'no' to anything. The only problem was his fear. Parents thought of getting some help from the school. They shared the problem with the principal of the school. The Principal loved children. When she called the child to her room, she was able to see the fear in the child's face. The child was so fearful as if he was called for some punishment. The Principal called the child near her and asked the parents to stay outside. She spoke to the child with lots of affection and asked about his daily routine. It was a surprise for the

You have to as I said so.

Principal how such a small boy can do so many tasks. He was fully disciplined. Lakshit even washed his clothes on holidays. He did all his work by himself. The Principal was feeling proud to have such a child in her school.

But when she wanted to know what made him do these work, she was shocked to know the real cause. Lakshit was quiet. When the Principal insisted on getting a reply, he mentioned that he has to do all these work irrespective of whether he is sick or fine. The reason which he mentioned shook the Principal internally. He mentioned that once after coming from school when he slept without completing his homework, his mother had beaten him very badly. Once his father thrashed him as he did not realise the time and came late from park. He shared many such instances. All these happened a few years back but each and every incident has been stored in Lakshit's memory in such a way that it seems as if those incidents of strict torturous discipline have occurred just today.

The Principal made the child sit outside with a few story books. Then, she called his parents and asked about the positive qualities of their child. They mentioned that he does all his work on his own. She praised them and asked, "How could you create such kind of discipline?" The parents tried to ignore the main issue and mentioned that since they themselves are so disciplined, their only child needs to be the same. Lakshit's father mentioned that each and every thing on his table is kept at the perfect place. No one can find out any fault. His mother also mentioned that she takes care of her job and home so efficiently that no one can point out anything. They were perfectionists and they wanted their child to be the same. So, they tried to do so by creating a fear of punishment. They formed rules but it was linked with physical punishment. Whenever the child was not able to stick to the rule, they used to beat him. This created fear in the child. He became anxious about his acts. His self-esteem deteriorated. There was no choice given to Lakshit. It was always "You have to because I say so..." He had no freedom or space of his own. His childhood was getting lost in the pressure of his parents' strict discipline.

When the Principal showed them the reality, it was difficult for the father to accept. But when he was able to see the effect of his disciplined lifestyle he felt guilty. His mother said, "I tortured my own son just because of my expectations."

Now the question was how to mend the whole situation. It was difficult to break the original habit pattern. But now his parents tried to link a positive feeling and a sense of achievement with this discipline. They started having discussions on how Lakshit felt when he did his work on his own. They stopped beating him and started having more positive discussions. Previously they used to focus on, "Why have you not done this?" "Why is this work left yet?" Now they started rewarding him verbally on the work which he completed efficiently. They started using more sentences like, "You are so systematic." "You complete your work all by yourself. It's amazing!" etc.

All these sentences helped Lakshit. He gained back his confidence. Sometimes he used to say, "I am feeling scared". But his mother responded with love, saying, "Yes, I understand. We will deal with this situation with courage." She never rejected his feelings. She acknowledged them and tried to reflect positivity through her statements. She understood that words can create magic and can work as therapy. So she started using positive words of encouragement in her discussions with Lakshit. His parents also stopped comparing him with their perfectionist habits. This created a relaxed atmosphere around the child.

It took time for Lakshit to come out of his fear. But he did it gracefully with his parents' help.

Summary:

Due to over expectation and faulty disciplinary patterns, there are a lot of negative emotions developing in children nowadays. We need to go deep into the problem. The reason as to why the child is fearful needs to be studied carefully. Parents should not ignore the problem. They need to study the environment and their own parenting style which might be creating the fear. Too much of authority in the parents damages the personality of the child. They need to be moderately authoritative so that the child has both discipline and breathing space. Moreover, it needs to be checked if anything around the child is causing fear. Effort should be made to enhance the self-esteem of the child.

09 Why can't I Control Myself?

Prashant, studying in class two, is in the limelight in his school. Everyone in the school knows his parents. They need no introduction, because they are called at least twice a week to hear complaint. He has become a matter of frustration for his parents. So they are thinking of putting Prashant in a hostel.

Though, he is small, his acts are big. He breaks tube lights in school and home; he can hit anyone any moment with anything. Recently he hit his friend with a pencil which just missed the friend's eyes. He throws caps of bottles of other children. His behaviour is unpredictable. He can remain quiet with a lot of

difficulty till an adult keeps an eye on him. But then he enjoys his freedom. He gets many such opportunities to celebrate his freedom. His mother's depression is evident in her eyes and his father has become so aggressive that any one can judge this while he opens his mouth.

Each and every member tries to control Prashant through various means. When he hits anyone, he gets thrashing from his teachers and his father. They feel that by beating Prashant they can show that they are doing justice to the child who was hit by Prashant.

Every day this vicious circle continued, Prashant being violent and the adults handling him more violent. Prashant's aggressiveness was increasing day by day. His handwriting was too bad. Prashant had difficulty in reading his own handwriting. When teachers used to teach in class, he would suddenly get up and ask permission to go to the toilet. They have no option other than saying 'yes' because they knew the unpredictable behaviour of Prashant and did not want to take any risk.

Soon Prashant's parents got a warning from the Principal of the school that he would be expelled if he commits any major mistake. The school had a system of providing a mentor for such children. The earlier mentor withdrew, as she was called for every mistake of Prashant. More than Prashant, she had to face social punishment. She had not heard about her own son as much as she heard "your Prashant did this, your Prashant did that". This challenge was too much for her which she could not take everyday. So another teacher was appointed for the task. The other teachers wished her which she took with a smile. Will she be able to handle Prashant with so much of pressure of her own classes? "Of course not", this was the opinion of all the teachers. They declared that Prashant is a gone case.

What helped Prashant and his parents?

The first thing, which Ankita madam (Prashant's new mentor) did, was to understand Prashant. She started the practice of story telling with Prashant. This helped Ankita madam to understand the underlying pain of Prashant. His stories revealed that he is not satisfied with adult members. In one story he shared that there was a child who used to beat others to check his strength as he wanted to take revenge from his father and teachers when he grows up. Every story had some reflection of Prashant's life. Ankita madam was touched by the stories. She realised that no one had tried to understand Prashant's pain, which worsened the situation.

Ankita madam soon found out that Prashant was interested in drawing and painting. So, she asked him to draw something and when she wanted him to explain what he had drawn, she was shocked to find that Prashant had compartmentalised his mother and father.

Too many questions were on her mind. "Do his parents stay separately?", "do they have frequent quarrels?", "do they disrespect each other?" She wanted to find out their answers.

In the mean time, there was a seminar in their school. A psychologist was taking session on behavioural problems. Ankita madam was sitting in the same seminar. Her mind was pondering over Prashant. Hopefully, she would get some clue. Out of many behavioural problems, one problem mentioned was ADHD (Attention Deficit Hyperactive Disorder). The symptom which was mentioned under this problem matched with that of Prashant. "Is Prashant suffering from ADHD?" Ankita madam thought. She wanted to go deep into the problem. After the session was over, she went personally to the psychologist and asked, "I want to know specifically about what is ADHD. Can you help me?"

The psychologist was ready to give her some time. They sat together and the conversation followed. She mentioned: "ADHD is a certain deficiency of neurotransmitter. This is a kind of neurobehavioral problem."

Ankita madam asked, "But how does one know that the child has ADHD?"

"This is indeed a very interesting question. The diagnostic guidelines also contain specific requirements for determining which symptoms indicate ADHD. These behaviours must appear early in life, before the age of seven and continue for at least six months. Above all, the behaviours must create a real handicap in at least two areas of a person's life, such as in the school, in the playground, at home, in the community, or in social settings. So someone who shows some

symptoms but whose schoolwork or friendships are not impaired by these behaviours would not be diagnosed with ADHD. Nor would a child who seems overly active on the playground but functions well elsewhere receive an ADHD diagnosis."

"Is there anything else which I need to notice to be sure that a child has ADHD?" Ankita madam asked.

The psychologist answered, "You can ask questions like, are these behaviours excessive, long-term, and pervasive? That is, do they occur more often than in other children of the same age? Are they continuous problems, not just a response to a temporary situation? Do the behaviours occur in several settings or only in one specific place like the playground or in the schoolroom?"

Ankita remained in constant touch with the psychologist so that she can do justice to Prashant.

It is important to understand a few terms related to ADHD.

Some signs of hyperactivity-impulsivity are:

- Feeling restless, often fidgeting with hands or feet, or squirming while seated
- Running, climbing, or leaving a seat in situations where sitting or quiet behaviour is expected
- Blurting out answers before hearing the whole question
- Having difficulty waiting in line or taking turns.

Inattention:

The DSM-IV-TR gives these signs of inattention:

- Often becoming easily distracted by irrelevant sights and sounds
- Often failing to pay attention to details and making careless mistakes
- Rarely following instructions carefully and completely losing or forgetting things like toys, or pencils, books, and tools needed for a task

- Often skipping from one uncompleted activity to another.

After knowing the symptoms, Ankita madam had to understand what could be done for Prashant. She realised that she cannot take care of Prashant alone. So, she started creating awareness in his parents.

His parents found it difficult to accept that Prashant had ADHD. They got a diagnosis done from a hospital before they were convinced of the issue. Things became easy for Ankita madam after the parents got the diagnosis done. They became very co-operative. From being "fed-up' they became "concerned". They realised that Prashant is doing things which are not in his control. He needs more love and affection and firm rules to deal with his problems. They helped Prashant in following simple rules like packing his bag, keeping his things in order and doing his homework, etc. For every rule which he followed, he was given points. This became a motivating factor for Prashant. His mother wrote the rules on a plastic board and pasted it on Prashant's almirah. This small technique helped Prashant to be disciplined in his daily works. At the end of the week, the points are counted and Prashant is gifted with a book of his choice. He generally prefers origami or art books.

His mother always had a fear of calling Prashant's friends home or to send Prashant to other places alone. Now, every week, she invites Prashant's friends so that she can observe Prashant in a social setting and also monitor his habit of hitting. She observed that Prashant becomes aggressive suddenly. He could not concentrate on one game for long. She gave the time-out punishment whenever Prashant became aggressive. This implied that Prashant was to be kept away from the group for two minutes. These two minutes seemed to be too long for Prashant. But on the other hand, Prashant was always given points for co-operating. This was done by speaking aloud.

Ankita madam was in constant touch with the psychologist. Even Prashant's parents had a session with the psychologist and found that their son needed medication. The psychologist instructed the parents that medication should only be taken under supervision of a clinical psychologist as this medication may demand change of doses due to minor side effects.

Indeed, behaviour therapy, social skills training, and medication helped Prashant. The most difficult task was to change the mindset of the teachers. Through these holistic approaches, the frequency with which the problems were occurring reduced. Moreover, he became a lovable child from a totally rejected child. His creativity in drawing was appreciated by the teachers which stimulated the positive emotions in Prashant.

ADHD children recover fast if they get more love, affection and firmness. Their problems aggravate, if they are seen as constant criminals. Following are the special guidelines for parents handling ADHD children:

1. Behaviour therapy would reduce problematic behaviour and create more desirable ones through a combination of positive and negative reinforcements. This can initially be done with the help of a therapist.

2. Fibre-rich diet is beneficial. Taking roughage and green vegetables would have a positive effect. Avoid junk and oily food. Chocolate and cold drinks are not good for children with ADHD. Also avoid artificially added chemicals such as colourings and preservatives.

3. A systematic time-table of the daily activities such as reading, eating, playing, etc. would help the child to be self-disciplined.

4. Encourage the child to participate in group activities and games.

5. To draw attention to a specific activity, encourage the child to copy some design/ diagrams as they are.

6. To improve concentration, encourage to do some yoga, exercises and meditation.

7. Head to toe exercises will help to eliminate toxin from the body and increase vitality. This can be done while listening to some interesting music.

8. Encourage eye contact to help the child be in track with the person he/she is talking to.

9. Watching television for a long time makes children irritable and aggressive. Therefore, T.V. needs to be avoided with positive reinforcement.

10. Parents need to handle such children with patience. Seeing a situation from a reactive frame of mind can somehow make things

look hopeless. Listening to the child with patience and then explaining in a calm voice would help.

11. Instructions should be precise and simple. Concentrate on what you are saying so that the child understands your language.

Summary:

Attention Deficit Hyperactivity Disorder (ADHD) is a condition that becomes apparent in some children in the pre-school and early school years.

Children with ADHD need consistent rules that they can understand and follow. If rules are followed, give small rewards. Children with ADHD often receive and expect criticism. Look for good behaviour and praise it. The earlier the problem is diagnosed, the better it will be to have early effect of treatment. Treatment may range from medication, behaviour therapy, social skills training, and parent/teacher orientation and counselling. These children need to be treated with special care as the behaviour problems are not under the control of the child. They are neurologically determined. The child may be in pathetic situation, if he is maltreated. So, people around need to understand the problem and give small responsibilities to the child to keep him engaged in a creative way.

I will not Leave You!

Mrs Rekha's seven-year-old son, Arpan, is becoming extremely violent and revengeful these days. If he feels that someone has lost his rubber, he would make sure that he throws the rubber of that child. The problem does not end here. His violence is even with non-living things. If he gets hurt by falling on the ground, he hits the ground with his foot with such intensity as if he wants to break the ground. His facial expression becomes so violent that no one can control him at that time. Now, Mrs Rekha is losing her patience. She had made him understand many a times that such behaviour is not acceptable but Arpan forgets everything within few seconds. The situation has become so bad that when Arpan shows such kind of behaviour, immediately, Mrs Rekha starts thrashing him. But nothing helps. The aggression in the family is increasing from all sides. Arpan's teachers are worried about his behaviour. They used to complain about his violent behaviour since nursery but these days it's almost regular that Mrs Rekha receives a call from some or the other teacher.

Violence among children is increasing in the present era. Parents compare their childhood with their own children and find a lot of difference in the behaviour pattern. There are many children like Arpan whose violence is a cause of worry for their parents. Parents try to look at the problems at a surface level. They do not look deep into it to deal with the problem. So, although they try various methods of making the child understand through various means, the child does not remember how to behave when the situation arises.

Let us first find out various causes of children's aggression:

1. Family problems: If there is problem or violence in the family, children may tend to develop violence.

2. Parenting style: If parents have been neglecting the child's emotional needs, it may hurt his self-esteem which may take any form, including violence.

3. Perception of neglect: If a child feels that he is being neglected in school or at home, he might feel frustrated and this frustration may lead to aggressive behaviour.

4. Not learning the positive way to seek attention: A child who is an attention seeker and does not find any constructive way to feel important, he/she might resort to unhealthy ways to seek attention. One such unhealthy way can be by showing aggression.

5. Pressure beyond tolerance: If the child is pressurised academically or in other ways to perform according to certain way, it can also accumulate feeling of frustration. A time will come when this frustration will turn into aggression.

6. Childhood training: If aggression was the only form in which parents solved the child's problems, the child would learn the same thing.

Parents can look deep and find many other reasons for the child's aggression. This needs to be dealt with as this problem may cause mishaps in future. The first thing which needs to be done is to find the root cause. Once we find the root cause of the problem, we can deal with it. Also, multiple things may work together to create the problem. So, we need to look at each and every aspect. When you look at the reasons behind Arpan's problem, you can deal with such kind of problems in a better way. So, let's go ahead and see what helped him and how.

What helped Arpan and his parents?

Arpan had a peaceful life full of attention till his mother delivered twin sons. This situation changed his mental state. Till now, he was getting all the attention from his parents. Although he used to be very active, his mother had all the energy to handle him with patience. This was one of the major reasons of Arpan's aggressive behaviour.

The other cause was, now his mother had to give some time to the other two kids. This was not acceptable to Arpan. Initially, he resisted his mother from taking the two kids, but later, he felt it was no use.

So, he accepted the fact outwardly but not internally. He felt that his mother's love was being shared between him and his twin brothers.

Another cause was faulty training. When Arpan used to fall on the floor, his parents, with lots of love, used to say, "Oh! Did this floor hit you? OK, don't worry we will hit it. You too hit." The aggression was given a shape at this stage. More than the love, comfort was provided by hitting. This kind of training in childhood creates problem for children at a later stage. How can such children, who have been trained in certain way, behave in some other way? They have learnt that whenever they get hurt, they need to hit back. So, a forgiving habit does not develop due to such kind of childhood training.

Arpan's parents were looking at all the problems at surface level till a new teacher came to the school and showed affection towards this child. Arpan had forgotten love and affection. He gets scolding at home and even at school. He was externally habituated to scolding but internally he was suffocated.

This new teacher called up Arpan's mother. The teacher showed her concern and also expressed her willingness to help Arpan.

It took some time for the teacher to understand problem. She realised that Arpan was pointed out when his behaviour was not good. But he did not get any specific clue as to find out what is the desired modified behaviour. He used to be asked, "Why do you hit?" or "Why can't you be good?" But Arpan was not so mature to understand what he could do to demonstrate good behaviour.

Now whenever Arpan hits anyone, the teacher calls him near her and asks what he could do to mend the situation. Arpan suggested various punishments as suggestions. He mentioned about standing out of the class, sitting on the floor for as long as the teacher wished, or not sending him for games period. It was as if Arpan is habituated to such punishments. So, this teacher immediately said, "No, I will not make you do all these as I know that you are a wonderful person. And I want the wonderful person in you to come out. See, Akshay (the boy Arpan had hit) is crying with pain. I know your words will be able to remove his pain. Let me see what you can do, so that he stops crying." She made Arpan go out of the class with Akshay while keeping a constant check on them. She saw Arpan holding Akshay's hand and saying sorry.

He tried to convince Akshay that he would not behave in this manner. The teacher was able to see a lot of affection in Arpan's conversation. This was what she wanted. After a while, Arpan came with Akshay. She asked politely and with a smile, "Are you friends now?" Akshay nodded his head. The teacher appreciated both the children for being friends. Then, she took Arpan with her to a room. She wanted to bring Arpan's positive feeling to the surface. She asked him how he was feeling after taking care of his friend. Arpan was not able to express his feelings in great detail, but he said in short and simple way, "Good madam".

The journey of correction started from here. The teacher shared her experience with Mrs Rekha who was surprised when she heard about Arpan's behaviour and realised that she should be more patient while dealing with her son. She realised that her child's focus needs to be redirected towards the desired positive behaviour. As she came to know the way, so experimenting became easier for her.

As was his habit, one day Arpan fell on the ground and started hitting the ground. His mother called Arpan near her and asked, "What has happened, Arpan?" Arpan said nothing but she could hear him breathing very fast. She said, "I understand Arpan, you are hurt. You are feeling bad that you fell." Arpan shouted, "No, this floor hit me." "But are you hurt?" his mother asked him. Arpan showed his knees and said, "See!" Honestly speaking, his mother saw no wound, still she empathised with her son and said, "I understand, let me kiss on your knee and you will see your pain vanish." It was difficult for Arpan to forget his old habit but still his mother was successful in calming him down.

She frequently started focusing on loving and taking care of his hurt rather than hurting others (living or non-living). Mrs Rekha was consistent in practising this way of redirecting. And amazingly, it helped! she felt that over a month she was able to see some change in Arpan's behaviour.

We should realise that when we work on the surface of any problem, it hides for some time but it recurs. But when we work on the root cause, the problem might take time to end, but it ends permanently.

Summary:

Aggression is increasing to a great extent in children these days. We find the reflection of anger at every place. But children learn aggressive behaviour through modelling. If parents can be calm in crisis situations, children also learn to do so. But still if the children demonstrate such aggression, it needs to be redirected towards the positive. Blaming and criticising the child will not help in dealing with his aggressive behaviour. Parents need to find out what sort of behaviour is required and then demonstrate the desired behaviour. Help the child to learn the positive behaviour pattern. Parents can also play some skits when the child is in a happy mood. This would change the negative behaviour of aggression into a calm and positive behaviour. But children should be made to practise the positive behaviour whenever they show aggression. Parents need to be calm at these moments. Children learn better when they are trained with calmness rather than aggression.

Where Have You Kept My Shoes?

Things were very fine till Arjav was small. His rude behaviour seemed to be sweet to all family members. Arjav's parents, Mr and Mrs Kaushik, used to praise him by repeating the tone in which he used to talk. Now, Arjav is in class V. The behaviour which was praised earlier has now changed into botheration. His parents are perturbed about his tone and language. He frequently uses language like: "Don't you know I need food after I come from park?", "How many times I need to tell you that I need colours?", "Where have you kept my shoe?" and "I am fed up of all of you", etc.

All these sentences are expressed in a harsh and rude manner. Parents were confused and they never realised how and when such a sweet child changed into an insulting kid. Arjav was academically brilliant. But his behaviour was problematic. He had formed his habit in such a way that he even insulted his parent in front of many guests. Initially his parents tried with polite methods, "Beta, why do you say in such a way? Can't you be polite? You will look so nice if you are polite." But Arjav remained the same. They then started handling him aggressively, saying, "We are telling you again and again. You will never listen. OK, from now, you will not go to park." Arjav used to say sorry several times and his wishes were fulfilled by the sentence, "But remember, if you do next time, we will not leave you." This approach helped them to get "sorry" word from Arjav but no "sorry" feeling.

Each one of us must have known one or two such kinds of children. The specialty of such problem is that these children are very intelligent. They are academically bright. So, sometimes they are forgiven for their

I am fed up
of all of you

misbehaviour. Due to the pressure of studies, parents sometimes ignore this kind of behaviour. Training is not provided from the beginning. Rather, children are rewarded initially.

Their words and sentences seem to be attractive. But later the same childhood rewards make the behaviour so strong that even when parents want to get rid of the behaviour, punishments do not work. The reason is that reward and reinforcement technique works better in strengthening the behaviour pattern than punishment. Punishment works temporarily, but the original behaviour may recur. Punishment may suppress the behaviour but is not very useful in long term.

Childhood training works better. So, a proactive approach may be taken for those children who are still young. While training any form of behaviour or language, the positive behaviour needs to be rewarded from the very beginning. Any sort of negative behaviour should never be rewarded despite the temptation of getting attracted to the child's sweetness and innocence. Parents ask, "What can the child understand now? We need to train him/her after he/she grows up." This is the biggest mistake. The child becomes confused at a later stage. All experiences of being rewarded get stored in the child's memory. So, he/she feels frustrated due to confusion. The child may internally think, "What is wrong with me now? I was like this before. But then, my parents were so nice. Now they have changed." This confusion makes the child more aggressive towards the parents. He/she (child) finds himself to be same, but has doubts about the credibility of his/her parents' behaviour. So, to avoid this confusion parents need to reveal what they would appreciate and what they would not. Children can read facial expression very well. Parents may convey what they like through their facial expression. Then, they can also redirect the negative towards the positive through means of diversion. Small children get diverted very easily. So, at that stage, diversion technique will work very well.

There is another aspect to this problem. The child learns better by observation. This is also called modelling. There are many families where some or other members talk in this tone. Either they are flat or they are rude. Children learn such behaviour. If the father or the mother, whom the child believes to be the role model, does not talk politely, the child learns the same to be the appropriate kind of behaviour. So, parents need to do what they want their child to do. Moreover, it will have double benefits. You will give a positive upbringing to your child and you will develop your personality and communication skills without paying any fees.

Another reason behind this behaviour pattern is when children depend on others for almost every work. If they do not work, they feel that it is not their responsibility. They will also not know what kind of management or skills the task needs. They would tend to be careless about things knowing that they would get the things needed by simply shouting. So, they might learn negative way of having a work done.

Parents need to train children to do their task themselves. It can start from a very small stage when children start going to school. If children are trained to keep ready their own dress, shoe, bottle, etc., a night before, it can give amazing results in future. These small responsibilities may create big outcome in future. But if these responsibilities are given when the child has grown up it causes frustration in the child. The child finds it difficult to adjust to the new rules and finds such a sudden responsibility as a punishment. They mention that parents do not have love for them now. Let the children carry their own bag too. Their self-esteem shows in their body language. Parents can also give positive stroke: "wow, you are very powerful. You can carry your bag yourself." These positive strokes would indeed be helpful for the child.

What helped Arjav and his parents?

Arjav was declared arrogant by all. His aggression was increasing day by day. His parents were concerned as they knew that he would not be able to adjust anywhere. But they had no solution to their problem.

When the summer vacation began, Arjav wanted to go to his uncle and aunt's place. His parents were confused whether to send him or not because they were sure Arjav would spoil all their reputation. Moreover, they were concerned that he would not be able to manage. Arjav's aunt used to remain ill. So, she would not be able to follow Arjavs commands.

But Arjav was stubborn and his uncle expressed his willingness to take Arjav to his place for 15 days. This period turned out to be a life-changing experience for Arjav's parents. Arjav returned with his uncle after 15 days. Arjav's mother was able to see a change in his eyes, they seemed to be calm than before. Arjav hugged his mother and went to his room.

Arjav's uncle wanted to speak to his parents. He mentioned about their difficulty in the initial days and how Arjav used to command everything. This was very irritating for them as they were not used to such kind of behaviour. The situation became so worse that they were thinking of sending Arjav back. But on the fourth day, Arjav's uncle became firm. He sat with Arjav alone and discussed all the rules and regulations of their family. Arjav frequently said, "It does not happen there." But his uncle firmly said, "But here we need to follow. And I am sure you can do wonders in following the system." He also mentioned that Arjav would be getting points from all in the house for doing his own work himself and how well he would do the work. It had amazing result. Arjav started cleaning his own clothes. Although the elder members of the family had to wash some of the clothes again as they were no so clean, but Arjav's effort was worth mentioning. He was praised for his efforts. His aunt frequently said, "I cannot believe that you never did your work. It seems you are habituated. You are simply great." Arjav realised how much effort it takes to do a work, how much care it takes to keep things at proper place and he learnt the basic values through these small acts of responsibilities.

Arjav's uncle shared one incident with his parents. One day Arjav was shouting at his aunt to give him some more vegetables. His aunt quietly said, "I cannot understand anything when anyone shouts. Can you please be polite?" She spoke this sentence in a polite but firm way. Arjav tried to misbehave but she did not say a single word. She called Arjav to the kitchen and said, "I know you can make me understand. Can you please be polite? You are such a wonderful person!" Arjav's voice changed at that moment.

They followed mix-and-match techniques to handle Arjav. But as Arjav was very intelligent he soon understood and learnt all the new method.

Arjav's mother was apprehensive whether this would work here but Arjav's uncle assured her to remove all her fears and practise these methods. It took some time but they really worked.

Summary:

Children can learn to be aggressive and arrogant due to various loopholes in the environment. First, we need to check our disciplinary style. If we are allowing children to shout and still listening to what they say, it encourages them to shout and get their work done. Second, if parents follow the same behaviour pattern, children learn those behaviours very fast through modelling. Third, children need to do their own work to feel the sense of responsibility. Parents may start with allowing their children to carry their own school bag. Respecting the work needs to be trained. This can be done only if children work on their own task. These children know how to handle their frustration of not having the work done. They have internal locus of control. They will be saved from criticising and blaming attitude.

Can't You Just Give a Remote Control Car?

Mrs Anju is highly tensed with her eight-year-old son, Harshit. He throws a lot of tantrums the moment he goes to the market with anyone. He has to be provided with something or the other. Before going to the market, he makes various agreements with his parents, but as soon as they reach there, Harshit forgets everything. One day it so happened that his mother did not have enough money to buy a ball which he demanded. He sat on the floor and started shouting and crying so much that his mother had to request the shopkeeper to provide her with the ball with the promise that she would bring the money soon. After coming back home, his mother yells at him and even beats him badly many times, but it is of no use.

Tantrum is a normal part of children's behaviour. It depends on the response of the parents whether it would reduce or increase. In most of the cases it has been found that parents want to deal with this tantrum but they surrender when the time comes. Many parents find great relief when the child is satisfied with a low-budget item while he demanded a very high-budget thing. But the main concern of dealing with gratification needs still remains. The child learns that if he demands anything, he would always get something. He also learns the strategies to fulfil his demands; he cries or shouts or sits on the ground. He also learns the limit of the parents, how much he has to cry or shout so that he gets his desired thing. Moreover, it has an impact in the future too. A tenth-class student, before his board exam, started throwing tantrums that he would not appear at his examination until he is provided with a bike. Parents had to give in to his demands because of the previous faulty training pattern. A child

I will not go until you give me the remote control car!
TOY SHOP

gets to know that if he wants a Mercedes, at least he is bound to get a Maruti 800.

Another disadvantage of not being able to handle the tantrum is that the child does not learn to postpone his desires or manage his desires if not fulfilled. This might cause behaviour problem in the future. If the child does not get something, he might resort to stealing at the adolescent stage. Thus it is better to take care of the tantrums when the child is small.

What helped Anju to deal with her child's problem?

One day Anju had gone to the market with her friend and her six-year-old son. In the market the boy saw a balloon and asked his mother whether he could get one. When Anju's friend firmly said no to her son, the child started in a low voice, "Mamma, just one. Please mamma, only one. Mamma it costs only five rupees." Anju saw that for a while her friend ignored her child's behaviour. Anju felt bad and she proceeded to the balloon seller to get one balloon. Her friend immediately stopped her and said, "Don't give him today as I have already said 'no'. Give him on some other day." Anju tried to convince her that it was just a matter of five rupees but her friend told her that it's just a matter of five rupees today but it will cost a lot in terms of behaviour at a later stage." Anju was convinced but still she waited to observe how her friend deals with her son's demand. The child kept on requesting his mother saying "Please, please" for sometime. Then the child started emotionally blackmailing his mother by saying, "You don't love me. If it would have been daadi, she would have immediately given me." Still she did not respond. After a few emotional dialogues, the child again started his requests. Now in a low, but firm voice, his mother said, "I do not like your behaviour. You know when I am saying no, it means no. By repeating your demand you are making me feel bad. I expect that you understand and we can talk about something else." The child kept on murmuring something. His mother repeated, "I am not appreciating your behaviour." Now the child was quiet. But Anju was surprised to see that the child became very normal and started sharing about how he won a game with his brother. Her friend was also normal and appreciated the child. They did not talk about the balloon after that.

Anju learnt a few lessons from the incident:

1. “No” should always remain a “no” despite any kind of pressure from the child.

2. No supplement should be given to compensate the original demand.

3. Lot of patience is needed when the child throws tantrum.

4. Sometimes the behaviour has to be ignored and sometimes it’s needed to express that the behaviour is not appreciable.

5. Appreciate such behaviour of the child which is worth appreciable.

When Anju reached home she was mentally prepared for her task. After a few days, she had to go to market with her son. This time, she was firm and told her son that if he demands anything, he will have to lose something he enjoys. This was slightly surprising for the child. Harshit was relaxed and hoped it was a part of his mother’s original anxiety. As usual, he went to the market and started demanding a remote-control car. This time Anju kept on doing her tasks like purchasing vegetables, and ignoring his demands. After a while, Anju said in a firm voice, “I am feeling very bad that you will not be able to go to the park today to play with your friends.” Harshit started arguing “But why?” Anju kept her patience and again said firmly, “If you keep on demanding something or the other, you will lose many things which you enjoy. It’s only the park now. There will be many more such things. I mean it.”

Harshit was confused. As per his habit, he shouted and cried but this time his demand was not fulfilled. Anju was feeling embarrassed as she felt all the passers-by are looking at her but she did not give up. She came back home. At five thirty p.m. Harshit started getting ready to go to the park. But Anju said, "You cannot go today Harshit and you know the reason. You have to play at home today." They struggled for 15 minutes. Anju felt many a times that she should allow him to go with a strict warning. But she was now able to visualise the benefit of her firmness for that one day. Although, it was one of the toughest day in Anju's life but this day made other days cool and relaxing for both Anju and her lovely son Harshit.

Summary:

Children know which strategy will work with whom. They try different strategies with different people to fulfil their demands. It is said that a child can be a better psychologist than a well- known psychologist. So, it's more challenging for the parents. They also need to learn various strategies to have a calm mental state.

When children throw tantrums, the first step is to be aware that the child is throwing tantrums and you need to stimulate your patience nerve. Thereafter, mention your decision and be clear about it yourself whether you wish to fulfil the desire or not. If yes, then, do not say 'no' first to show your power. Say yes immediately. If you have to say 'no', stick to it till the end. You can use various strategies like diversion (try to divert the child to other interesting events), ignoring, or firmness in expressing that you do not like such kind of behaviour, or alternative punishment If you are stating any alternative punishment, be sure that you can apply it. It should be realistic. Punishment should not be physical punishment. If you can think about alternatives, you would find end number of possibilities to handle the tantrums of your child by changing your own response pattern.

BILE
STORE

I need a Personal Mobile

***A**rpit needs a personal mobile phone. He is twelve-year-old and studies in class VII. He has all the logic behind his demand, "My friends have it. After all didi (his elder sister) has a personal mobile. He argues with his parents why he can't have one when they can afford. Mrs Kanchan is confused whether she should give her son a personal phone or not. She sometimes feels that it is injustice. She should not deprive her son just because of a mobile. Arpit cries for the mobile everyday. He does not talk politely. His behaviour is becoming worse day by day. "What is the harm?" says Mr. Kaushik. But Mrs. Kaushik is scared. One part of her self says "yes" while the other part says "no".*

Owning a personal phone has become a fashion in today's modern society. Parents feel it is important to give a phone to their children. Many parents give because they want to be kept informed, many give because they do not want their child to feel inferior, and others give to avoid the tension at home.

Children, who get the mobile phone, get so involved in the mobile phone and enjoy the company of the phone but they get far away from their parents. Think about the irritation we have when any of our family members talks over the phone for a long time. Bonds tend to decrease even if adult members are talking over phone most of the time.

The other problem may be when the parents lose track of their child. The child remains busy with the phone. There are many students who mention that they feel depressed when their friends do not pick up their calls. They also feel rejected when no one calls them. They cannot share these things with their parents. When parents ask about their withdrawal behaviour pattern, they get irritated and burst out at their parents. At this stage, the parents find it difficult to take away the phone. Children start getting habituated to the phone. Breaking the habit is difficult for all. It takes a lot of internal control. But when a habit is tried to be changed with external control, it is even more difficult.

There also have been cases where children get sexually oriented jokes from their friends. Most of them delete it immediately with the fear of being caught but those jokes get stored in the memory of the child. This creates problem in concentrating in constructive things as they feed their mind not with something positive. Sexual feelings or romantic feelings are common in adolescents but sexual jokes or sexual talks can be harmful. These children tend to view the world with their own eyes. They become "black listed" in the school. Respect starts missing from their eyes.

Many students get caught in the school with mobile phone which destroys the image of the child. The child lives in the school with the fear of being caught. Thus, it becomes difficult for the child to concentrate in the class.

Controlling children's talking habit is very difficult. Students are filled with so much to share that they find talking a never-ending process. They need money to talk over phone and for money they need to depend on parents. So, it becomes an unending process. There are many students who tell that they have installed some scheme-based connection. They talk the whole night without sleeping and thus avoiding school in the morning.

Just one decision of giving a mobile can invite a big basket of problems. Is it worth?

But then, what can parents do? Is there any solution? Yes, there is. Each problem has a solution if given proper attention. It may be a long process and may need effort but the outcome would always be positive.

What helped Arpit and his parents?

Arpit needed personal space in everything. His parents did not want to give him a personal mobile but felt that they had no choice. Aggression was increasing from Arpit's side. They tried to convince Arpit in some way or the other. The more they tried to convince, the more his aggression increases. At last his mother decided to give him a personal mobile on his birthday. Just one week before the birthday, there was a parent-teacher meeting in his school. But this time it was different for Mrs Kanchan. She was standing to take the feedback of her son's performance while the teacher was talking to a group of parents. Mrs Kanchan was spellbound on hearing the conversation. She got to know that these students are bringing mobile in the school and passing on jokes with sexual connotation to each other. They were caught when their bags were checked. Three students who were caught had all sexual material stored in their phones. Parents shared that these children do not allow parents to touch their mobile. It was obvious. Why would they? The performance of each was deteriorating. This was also obvious. How can they concentrate with such kind of "sexual thought paralysis"?

All those parents decided in front of the teacher that they would take away the mobiles from their children. The teachers also took an administrative decision that these children's section would be changed. So, these children were separated from the group with whom they were since childhood. Due to the ignorance factor from parents, these students faced several punishments: first punishment was their image damage, second punishment was insult and scolding from teacher, third was harsh and painful punishment from parents, fourth was destruction of their self-esteem. Will this damage be wiped out? Perhaps no! These students might have to bear with the name of "dirty students" for their whole lives. Maybe others would not say it in words but they would see it in the eyes of others. Even when others forget about whole episode, it will be stored in the episodic memory.

Mrs Kanchan was now convinced about what she had to do. She came to know that adolescent children find it difficult to see the long-term impact of such mistakes. But she was able to see it. She found it easier to handle the momentary aggression than the long-term damage.

Now, she became firm. She made Arpit sit in front of her and shared her fear. Arpit wanted to convince her but she was firm. She also said that she would not like to talk about this topic again as she would not give a mobile. But apart from this topic, Mrs Kanchan started giving more time to Arpit and started sharing about many thing with Arpit. This created a bond between Arpit and Mrs Kanchan. Whatever she wanted to give, she gave without using the power of a "mother" by saying "no" and then "yes". If Arpit asked something, and she could give, she gave immediately or said "yes" immediately. If she needed time to think, she shared the same by saying: "Arpit I would need some time to decide."

This sharing and being firm on certain issues helped Mrs Kanchan to create a healthy bond with Arpit. Arpit is now happy with his family and his materialistic needs have also reduced.

Summary:

The moment children start being materialistic parents should go beyond the material and understand the need of the child. If the child wants a fashionable item to take to school, they should find the reason behind this need. Is it to seek importance? Is it to tease other children? Is it to create friendship with someone? Once you understand the need, you can try to fulfil the need in a constructive manner. A need will never be bad but the way children want to fulfil the need can be damaging. The more quality time we give to the children, the more we listen to them, the more we shall be able to build up a bond with them. Their materialistic clinging would reduce naturally. The earlier we begin, the better it would be. In certain cases, if we feel that certain things would have a lot of damage if misused, it is better to be firm and convince the child why you cannot give the thing. Answer all "whys" during that personal time, however if the child is continuously talking on the same topic, say that you do not like it. If you wish you can tell him, "We have already talked on this issue. If you wish we can sit in the evening and talk about it again. But now, I will not like to talk on this issue." Be firm in your statement and see the magic. But do not snatch away your affection. Shower him with affection and genuine appreciation.

14

Mamma, Papa, You Only Love My Brother!

Akshita, the seven-year-old daughter of Mr and Mrs Sharma, has become very irritating these days. She keeps on comparing herself with her four-year-old younger brother, Aman. She fights regularly with him for some reason or the other. She pulls her brother's hair and one day even dragged her brother out of the bed. Aman fell on the floor and he cut his forehead. The parents feel scared to leave both of them alone at home even for half an hour. They sometimes try to make her understand the love between a brother and a sister. In response Akshita says that they just favour Aman. They only love Aman. Her parents try hard to prove that they love both of them but just after five minutes, fight between the two resumes. They even beat Akshita to make her feel her mistake. This has led to a

frequent hostile environment in the family. Akshita is convinced that her parents do not love her, and they only love her brother Aman.

Lot of parents are upset with such kind of sibling rivalry and are worried about how to deal with such situation. They make every effort to give fair judgment but it has no positive effect. The parents also worry about whether such aggression will remain forever. A lot of energy is wasted in handling such situations. Many times the mother, who has to look after the household activities as well, gets irritated and she feels confused about who is right and who is wrong. This makes the situation worse. If the judgment is given in favour of one child who is wrong, the other one becomes very violent. Parents feel that it is a part of their life and they have to bear this permanently. The damage is not till here. The healthy relation of the siblings totally ends up. They try every means to let down and find fault in the other child. Even when the same things are brought for both of them still they feel that other one is better than his/her. Parents make every effort to make them feel that they are treated equally. Once Mr Sharma stopped talking to the elder one for few days stating that she would only start talking once she behaves politely with her younger sibling. The child did try to behave so but there was artificiality in the behaviour.

Most parents fail to find the real cause. They focus on the behaviour of the children but never analyse their own behaviour, which can be one of the major cause of such rivalry.

What helped Akshita, Aman and their Parents?

This tense scenario was building up in the home. Everybody had become mechanical in their behaviour. The mother used to beat both of them after every few minutes. The relation between the parents has also worsened. They started blaming each other for the misbehaviour of their children.

One day, when Akshita and Aman were fighting, their mother was taking rest. She was so fed up with such situations that she did not go to deal with the situation. She could hear both of them shouting and complaining about each other, "Mamma, *didi* is taking my toy", "Mamma, Aman has broken my pencil", etc. Mrs Sharma kept her calm although she was felt that she should get up and thrash both of them. But she was so tired that she did not have the energy to get up.

For fifteen minutes she was able to hear them shouting. After some time when she could hear no noise she was even more scared. When she could no longer stop herself she got up and went to the other room. To her surprise she found them playing chess. She could not stop herself from saying, "I am so happy to see you playing so nicely!" This time she was able to see a different expression. She saw both of them having a glance towards each other with a sweet smile. She felt the love for both the child. She hugged both of them together and sat with them to observe their game. Instantly, there was a bond of love amongst the three of them.

Mrs Sharma finally found a way out! She learnt to ignore the negative behaviour and encourage the positive behaviour. Now she felt that it is better to motivate and appreciate them together when they are behaving well.

Mr Sharma also found another way. One day just as he had come back from office, Akshita and Aman came running with their complaints as usual: "Papa, *didi* had beaten me today also", "Papa, Aman was cheating in the game". This time he acknowledged the feelings of both without giving any judgment. He asked each of them to share one positive feature of the other child and mentioned that he would be able to listen to them only if they shared one positive feature of the other and one negative point about self. Both were silent for some time and looked at each other. After some time they could mention the positive features in each other. Their father immediately appreciated both of them for this. But while searching for one's own negative factors, it was indeed difficult. It took some time.

Initially they started with, "Actually when *didi*..." Mr Sharma immediately stopped them. He told that whatever the other person has done, he has to mention a negative point about one's own. It was not easy for them but they did it. However, they did not like it. But he reminded them of the appreciation which they did for each other. This created a positive atmosphere. Moreover, both were happy that there was no judgment this time.

Mr Sharma did it unknowingly as he had failed in all other approach. He was not aware whether this technique would create a positive

bond between the siblings or not but certainly he was feeling much better as a father. This brought about a lot of positive feelings in both of them. Although Akshita and Aman did not stop fighting and quarrelling but the anxiety and artificiality was reduced. Once when Mrs Sharma was scolding Aman for a mistake immediately Akshita came and accepted that it was her mistake and not her brother's. Mrs Sharma felt great that her children had not only started taking responsibility for their positive behaviour but also for their mistakes.

Summary:

Parents can never deal with sibling rivalry by trying to be a judge. They can only succeed by acknowledging their positive behaviour. While any kind of rivalry is going on, they need to mention without judgment that they are not feeling good about the whole issue. If need be, they can separate the siblings for some time. This would give time to each one to understand the situation. Children would always want to be together. After a while they would request parents to allow them to be together. This sort of time-out punishment has universally been proved to be very effective. When siblings are being friendly towards each other, parents can share their joy and can join them. This is a wonderful opportunity to create emotional bond with children. Parents would be able to see the benefit of such efforts at a later stage of their life. If children are quarrelling for a toy, it is better to ask them if they can share and maintain peace. If not, parents can keep the toy away from their reach and tell that if they cannot share, no one would play with the toy. They would realise their loss and would try to mend such negative behaviour. This would not bring jealousy but would develop a sharing habit. Even for TV programme, if there are different choices, there can be prior discussion. Discussion might take some time but it will have lots of mental peace in the long-term. After the discussion, parents need to stick to the mutually agreed decision. Remember, parents need to find a way out so that siblings are positive towards each other today and even tomorrow.

15 Why Should I Say Sorry?

Mr and Mrs Singhal are worried about the long-term effect of their nine-years-old son Rishav's behaviour of never admitting his mistake. He has every excuse for his mistakes. His statements are mostly like: "Actually, ma'am rubs the board so soon that I was not able to write", "The glass of water fell from my hand because of you. Why did you call me at this moment?", "I had to beat him as he was shouting on me. I had no choice, etc." He will never say 'sorry'. When pressurised to say sorry, he would ask with a strange look, "Why? It was not my fault! Why should I say sorry?" He shouts when someone asks him to say sorry. He leaves the scene by saying, "You people always let me down! You all are bad." Mr Singhal, well aware of the business and job environment, feels scared when he imagines the difficulties his son would face in future.

There are many children who develop such a habit of giving excuses. This is not a problem only for their present, but will also cause lot of problems in their future. They even create problems in others' life. They develop blaming tendencies along with giving excuses. Infact, this tendency to blame is the side effect of the 'excuse giving habit'. Children like Rishav also face difficulties in school. They feel that the teachers are partial and other children are selfish. In the long run, these children tend to become lonely, attention-seeking and aggressive. They are always in the teachers' complaint lists. When they enter the job environment, they become the most hated person because of their continuous blaming and criticising attitude. They even lose interest in those works which demand interaction with others. As a result, they become poor team players.

It is better to take care of any such problem when the child is small and it is easy to change his habits. Rishav's parents tried to deal with this problem by pressurising him to say sorry. Generally Rishav succeeded in getting his own way. But when he had to say sorry, he said it mechanically. Rishav felt insulted. He was pressurised to say sorry and this led to other negative behaviour in him. He started making fuss while eating; he felt that his mother intentionally makes food which he doesn't like.

His parents knew that this behaviour is creating problem and tried to deal with the problem but in a negative way. This negative dealing (pressure) was generating more negatives from Rishav's side. "What else could we do?" was the father's statement. "He doesn't listen! He is so adamant! We are fed up of him!"

A child is intelligent and knows what his/her parents feel and think about him. He gets the vibration of his parents being fed up of him. A gradual and distant relation was automatically created between Rishav and his parents.

What helped Rishav and his parents?

As the days turned worse, Rishav's aunt came to visit the family. She was a calm and composed lady. Rishav liked her a lot. One day Rishav was not able to find his toy. He started blaming the maid that she had stolen it. Knowing his attitude, the maid remained quiet but his mother started shouting at him. Rishav also raised his voice. Aunt Neera observed the whole situation and she quietly said,

"I know Rishav, you can find your things very soon. I am sure you will get it within five minutes. Remember the last time I came, I did not find my spectacles and you searched it for me!" There was a tone of appreciation in Aunt Neera's voice and a sweet smile on her face. Rishav felt proud of himself as he recalled the event. "Let us both search and let us see who succeeds! Please this time, let me win." There was a change in action. From shouting, Rishav immediately became active in searching his toy. Aunt Neera asked him to describe the toy so that she could also search it. Both of them enjoyed the process. Who won? Obviously Rishav! Moreover, Aunt Neera wanted him to win. Rishav was very happy to win. Aunt Neera appreciated his effort by saying, "I am so happy that you have won. You are really great!" Mrs Singhal observed that Aunt Neera did not force Rishav to apologise in front of the maid. After a while, when the maid was leaving, Rishav opened the fridge and took out few toffees and handed out four toffees to the maid saying, "Please give two to each of your children." The maid smiled and put her hand on Rishav's head. For the first time she was able to see Rishav's positive behaviour towards her. She was indeed very happy.

In the evening when the family was having snacks together, Aunt Neera said, "You know this maid leaves her two kids to take care of your house. She cleans your house so that you can feel good in it. I felt so good that you thought about her sons. I am sure God will take care of you when you take care of people around you. Moreover, your behaviour seemed to be so nice when you were giving those toffees. The children must be so happy to have those toffees. They rarely get such things."

Rishav's mother observed that Aunt Neera was continuously highlighting only the positive behaviour which was around one percent according to her. She was ignoring the bad words which Rishav uttered. But Mrs Singhal did not want to interfere in between because she was feeling good about the whole interaction. She realised that the behaviour which would be highlighted would get repeated, as she was constantly focusing on the negative behaviour in an effort to mend them, they were getting repeated.

At around 8.00 p.m., when Rishav's father came from his office he started enquiring his wife, "Did you give milk to Rishav? Did he go to his dance class?" Rishav's mother replied with an irritation in her voice. When he went to the bed room and found that Rishav's books were scattered on the bed, he immediately shouted at his wife, "You are so careless. Didn't you see the books scattered here? I don't know what you do for the whole day!" Mrs Singhal now burst out sarcastically, "Yes, you remain for the whole day and do all the cooking and other household works. I have to even go to pay the electricity bill." All these happened in front of Rishav.

Aunt Neera found the root cause behind Rishav's behaviour. She realised that Rishav has developed this faulty habit from his parents. When Rishav went to bed at night, she discussed the issue with them. They too wanted to rectify his behaviour. But they could find no way out. Both keep on blaming and criticising each other. Rishav is learning such negative behaviour pattern as children learn faster from what they see than what they hear.

It was difficult for both of them to get away with their blaming tendencies but since they were concerned about their son, they tried to change themselves. They became aware of their mistakes and so each time they blamed each other, they tried to find the fault within themselves. Aunt Neera had told them to be aware of their own mistakes and correct them.

After around one month, it became their habit to apologise whenever they commit some mistake or whenever they hurt the other person. Rishav initially used to feel strange but he felt good. Once he was surprised to see that his father said sorry to his mother as he had forgotten to bring something which his mother had asked for. But whatever happened increased the "feel good" factor in their home. Now Rishav also feels comfortable to admit his mistakes. It took some time but he did learn when his mother also said sorry when she scolded him because of her own irritation. Previously, she used to say, "You irritated me and so I had to scold you." But now she started saying, "I was feeling irritated inside, so I scolded you. I am so sorry Rishav. I should not have done so. I will check myself from now." Rishav has also learnt to say, "Its O.K. mamma."

Summary:

Ups and downs are a part of every person's life. But these ups and downs should not have a negative effect on a child's behaviour pattern. Children learn to blame and develop the tendency to give excuses from their environment. They even learn such negative behaviour pattern due to the fear of punishment. First, parents need to check what negative behaviour is going on in the child's surrounding environment. Second, parents also need to check whether they punish or scold the child even when he/she child is accepting his/her mistake. If so, the child will soon learn to give excuses and blame others. Parents need to praise whenever the child accepts his mistake. It is important to make the child realise that it is alright to have mistakes but it is also important to learn from the mistakes and to take the responsibility to rectify the mistake.

So, if the child drops something, parents may quietly say, "Its O.K. Take the wiper or duster and clean the place." After the child cleans, appreciate him for his effort. But here parents need to be firm. If the child checks his mistake once, chances are that he will learn fast. Discuss the values when the child is in a calm state of mind as Aunt Neera had discussed the maid's effort.

Why am I so Anxious?

Shaina, studying in class V, is a brilliant and a smart child. She participates in many extra-curricular activities and gets lots of prizes in any written competition she participates. But despite her smartness, she is never able to stand first due to her anxiety. She gets tensed when she has to go on stage and her anxiety shows on her face. Her voice modulation is wonderful, but she seems to be mechanical on the stage. Many times she forgets things. She cries after she loses. She had even given the interview for the junior head girl in her school but was not able to make it due to her anxiety.

Her dreams remain unfulfilled due to her anxiety. Her parents are not worried about her not getting awards but about her anxiety. Shaina repeatedly asks her parents, "Why this always happens with me? Why I can't be the head girl? Why God makes me nervous on the stage?" They try to focus on all her positive features, but Shaina remains dissatisfied with all those explanations.

This is a different case where the child has her self-imposed expectations. There is no pressure from the parents, in fact they try to give a lot of space to her but Shaina is not ready to accept any consolation for her self-perceived defeats. She has established her success criterion: to be first while performing on stage. Her frustration increases when she observes that she is not able to perform well despite all her preparations.

Shaina was loved and appreciated by everybody during her childhood. As and when she grew up, she realised that this unconditional love is based on her performance. Since a very small age, she tried to do her best in her studies. She found that she was getting the rewards by being focused in her studies. Gradually, as her education process progressed, she observed other students getting appreciation through various stage presentations. Whenever anyone got any prize, teachers appreciated that student and made other students clap for him/ her. Her friend who won various prizes by performing on stage was appreciated even in the school bus by various students and teachers. Shaina also wanted the same thing for herself and wanted everybody to praise her.

As a result she became over-focused on getting appreciation. And in the process, she lost track of the process. While performing she had a high level of anxiety on winning and she started repeating these sentences often: "I have to win", "I have to win", "What if I don't win?", "No, not this time, I cannot take it anymore". Thus, these statements over-ruled her. She never understood how she was drowned under the strong waves of these over-anxious statements. She was not aware of this internal anxiety. Whenever anyone asked her whether she was feeling nervous, she used to say, "No, I am fine."

Will her dream always remain a dream? No! Where there is will, there is a way.

What helped Shaina and her parents?

Shaina's frustration was increasing and her interpersonal skills were getting damaged day by day. Her anxiety was getting reflected in other aspects of her life. She had a role model, named Sakshi, who was the head girl of senior school. Her motive behind making Sakshi her role model was due to Sakshi's confidence in her stage appearances.

Once there was a programme in the school where she had to work with Sakshi in a play. Shaina was over-enthusiastic to be the best out of all the groups while Sakshi was very calm and composed. She said, "Shaina, we will do our best and let us also learn to appreciate others." Shaina did not express that she did not like the sentence. In the middle of the work, Shaina asked, "*Didi* what if I forget?" Sakshi looked at her and replied softly, "So what?" Shaina was surprised, "Don't you want to win?" Sakshi replied that she wants to win but also understands that there might be some unexpected problem, the management of which is more important than winning. No one spoke to Shaina in this way. Sakshi explained how she forgot her dialogue when she was in class IX. But she had asked the audience to give her some time to recall. She thanked God for bringing such a situation in her life which taught her how to handle such embarrassing situations.

"Great! But what about teasing by friends?" asked Shaina. Sakshi quietly replied, "Then you are learning two things: one how to handle audience when you forget and how to handle your friends." Shaina felt good being with Sakshi. It was as if some power was getting transferred to her through Sakshi.

On the day when they had to present the play in front of the entire school and parents, Shaina's parents were also present. They went to the dressing room where Shaina was with Sakshi and were surprised to see that she was singing some Hindi film songs with Sakshi (being a sensible girl, Sakshi did it deliberately to reduce Shaina's anxiety). And it worked. Shaina was diverted from her anxiety to a relaxed state. She came running to her mother and asked her, "Mamma, look how am I looking? See I have put lipstick like you. Am I looking like you?" her mother replied with joy in her heart, "No, you are looking better than me." When Shaina embraced her, she said, "Be careful Shaina, your makeup will get spoiled." But Shaina was feeling comfortable holding her mother.

When the show began, as per her habit, Shaina's face reflected her tensions. But when Sakshi came running and stood beside her and told her to smile, she started smiling, looking at others. Shaina wanted to take away her tensions and so she had asked her to smile.

At any kind of stage show it is important to come out of the self-focus thinking pattern. Only then can one perform with confidence.

Just before her show Sakshi took Shaina to a room away from the stage and made her shout, "I have prepared well and I will do well." There was no competition feeling injected through this statement. Shaina was feeling better. It was as if some heavy burden went out of her body.

This is an excellent technique to manage anxiety and anger. Frame a positive sentence like "I will complete this chapter today and I can" and shout loudly. Check your feelings. You will feel great.

This time Shaina presented the show with adequate facial expressions and good voice modulation. She enjoyed performing this time. After

coming out of stage, there was a smile on her face which said, "Yes, I did it." And yes, she did it!

Shaina was declared the "best voice modulator". Her team got the first prize. This prize was an additional bonus for her. She ran to Sakshi and said, "*Didi* thanks." Sakshi was surprised. Shaina continued, "*Didi* I learnt a lot from you. From now on, I will enjoy the performance rather than thinking of being first." Sakshi gave her a smile and put her hand on Shaina's cheek with affection and said, "You are extremely talented. I did nothing. You had all within yourself." Sakshi was modest enough to say this and perhaps this is the reason that she is the head girl. A leader tries to bring out the true potential of other people and Sakshi did the same. Perhaps Shaina would never forget Sakshi. She would remain in her memory for her whole life. Whenever Shaina went on stage, she whole- heartedly remembered Sakshi.

During the entire week after the programme, Shaina narrated to her parents the small moments she had with Sakshi. Her parents were very happy to see the change in her. They understood that while they were using lectures to change her, Sakshi did it through her behaviour. Her mother realised that she is also a perfectionist and gets tensed over any minor mistake. She hates people pointing out her mistakes and whenever such a thing happens, the anxiety shows on her face. So she decided to work on her behaviour as well.

Summary:

There are many children who have a fear to go on stage. It is useless to convince them by saying that their fear is baseless. To some extent, fear is normal. Even the best of speakers feel butterflies in their stomach before they go on stage. In fact, it is normal and gives them a push to perform with full enthusiasm. So parents, rather than taking the child's moderate anxiety in a negative way, should say, "It is good that you are slightly anxious. This will help you perform better since you have prepared well." Moreover, talking about other interesting things also relaxes the mind. Sometimes, listening to songs also helps in taking away the attention from oneself. And the ultimate thing is to appreciate the effort of standing and speaking on the stage more than getting the prize. Parents also create high level of expectation on winning. Instead the focus needs to be on enhancing confidence level while standing on the stage. Nothing is better than an increased self-esteem.

I Cannot Sleep

Everything was fine with nine-year-old Swasti till last month. Since then she has developed a strange problem of not having sound sleep at night. Her parents are very worried and need to wake up with her every night. She sleeps for maximum one hour and then wakes up. She then wants to talk to her mother. Since her mother is a working lady, it becomes difficult for her to remain awake at night. Swasti, herself is also worried. She too wants to sleep well at night because it becomes a problem for her to wake up in the morning and she can not even concentrate in school.

What could be the problem? When will she recover? Doctors believe it is psychological and they need to consult a psychologist. Let us now focus our attention on Swasti and see whether she is able to get sound sleep at night or not.

Days went by and her parents became more and more worried about her behaviour. Many a times, they felt that she is doing it deliberately. Their scolding, love and affection had no effect. They could not make her sleep at night.

Sleep is very important for all of us. We re-gain our energy after a good sleep. At night, the body produces more hormones that stimulate growth. It is important to note that every child has a unique pattern of sleep. A pre-school child normally sleeps for ten to twelve hours each day, whereas a school-going child sleeps for approximately ten hours each day. If there is a slight fluctuation in this pattern, parents need not worry as far as the child is happy and healthy. But if the child sleeps too much or too less and also has some behaviour problem, the child needs care and concern.

We feel very irritated after one night without sleep. After months without sound sleep, Swasti, too, has become irritable, rude and her behaviour is very demanding. She is dull all the time. Besides, one member not sleeping creates a problem for the whole family.

What helped Swasti and her parents?

Swasti was taken to a psychologist who tried to build up a rapport with her. Swasti always wanted to talk to people and so this helped her to vent out her feelings. But she was not very clear about the reason behind her problem. At the surface level she seemed to be satisfied but the psychologist knew that there must be something hidden inside. So she tried to find out this. She became a good friend of Swasti and gradually came to know of several problems:

- Swasti never sleeps at a specific time. Sometimes she sleeps at 9.00 p.m., sometimes at 10.00 p.m. and sometimes even at 12.00 p.m. Her sleeping time depends on her parents' work schedule. She insisted on sleeping with her parents, and since her mother used to work and father came late from office, there was no scope of going to bed early. But she has to wake up early since she has to go to school.

- Her mother could rarely give her time and talk. So, her anxiety made her wake up at night and cling to talk to her mother.

- Before sleeping, Swasti watches television. So she is never in a relaxed mood before sleeping.

These things about Swasti helped the psychologist to deal with the problem. So she motivated Swasti and her mother to change their life style and interaction pattern.

Within just 15 days it was possible for Swasti to sleep with a relaxed mind and her parents were also relieved.

How was it possible?

1. Swasti's mother thought previously, "It is just not possible to go to bed at a particular time." But now she was able to see a ray of hope if she changes her statement to "How can I make it possible?" Gradually she was able to go to bed with Swasti at 9.00 p.m., chatting with her

for few minutes till Swasti closed her eyes with a relaxed state of mind. This helped Swasti in two ways: first, she was able to get her mother's company and second, she was able to vent out her accumulated feelings. So, while sleeping, she was in a relaxed mode.

2. Her mother started monitoring her habit of watching the TV. She started playing more games which could exhaust her brain energy. Her father started playing games like chess, carom board, etc. with her. These helped her in two ways. First, rather than just watching TV for long hours and straining her eyes now she was into constructive thinking. Second, she was naturally building a bond with her father. Her parents started discussing with her about her favourite things. She agreed that she would be watching T.V. only on weekends for half an hour.

3. She became more involved in physical activity every day. She started going to the park to play with her friends. Sometimes her parents used to dance along with her, playing fast music. It proved to be a relaxation therapy for her and she loved these moments.

Gradually, there was more interaction between her and her parents through games, studies, discussions and other activities.

Summary:

Sometimes our sleep may be disturbed not because of any physiological reason but due to psychological reasons. When such a thing happens, doctor needs to be consulted. If physiological factors are ruled out, then the child needs to be dealt with psychologically. Some of the following tips can be of help to parents:

a) Give lots of unconditional love to the child.

b) Interact positively with the child combined with appreciation and valuing his/her opinion.

c) Change of life style by reducing activities which are likely to increase internal anxiety.

d) Create a positive environment in the home.

I don't Want to Go Out to Play

Mohit is always so quiet! He does not talk to anyone. He sits in his room and keeps on looking outside the window of the room. His parents are concerned because it has been three months since this drastic change has occurred in their six-year-old son. They try to talk to him but are unable to find out the reason behind the change in his behaviour. Mohit just answers in 'yes', 'no' or 'hmmm'. He was an energetic kid full of charm just three months back when they used to stay in their old house.

What could have happened? Both parents were worried about this sign of absent mindedness in Mohit. He started remaining quiet even in school. He seems to be lost in his own world. Parents tried to talk to him but he shares that he doesn't understand what is happening. He simply replies "I am not feeling like....".

Usually it so happens that when parents look for a new house, they completely ignore the training part of children. This gap in turn creates a problem in the future. Growing children are very sensitive about their surroundings, friends, home and neighbourhood. They are not only attached to people but also to the walls of their homes. So, a sudden shift in the environment may cause a lot of psychological trauma for them. It may sound simple for parents as they would be busy in re-setting the new house, but for the little child it may be a big loss.

Certain things need to be taken care of before choosing a new house. Parents need to take into consideration their child and talk to the child, share his/her ideas and then generate ideas in the child's mind. This would create a better psychological mindset in the child who would, in turn, feel important as well create a positive feeling towards the new house.

Further, it is seen that many parents take their child along while they are searching for a new house. As a result the child forms perceptions about the positives and negatives about the new place when they hear it being discussed on front of them. So, the problems which the parents discuss about the new house enters into the child's mind and therein the anxiety starts. The child does not have much say in the decision making. So, whatever he shares does not make any impact. Parents neglect his words by saying, "You need not worry. You would not have any problem. And learn to adjust."

So it is better if the child does not hear about the evaluation of the new home. When the parents have made the final decision, the child needs to be told about various other things like his new school, new surroundings, new friends as well as how the old friendships can be maintained. The transition to the new place would need time. So, it is important to make the child aware of the positive features about the new place.

It is also important to listen to what the child talks about and answer his questions time and again. It is better to ask the child, "Tell me what you desire", "How do you want things to happen?" etc. When the child can think of a solution, he is much more relaxed and confident.

These things would be helpful before taking any choice/ decision of a new house. Let us now see what can be done to come out of a situation like Mohit.

What helped Mohit and his parents?

Days passed by and Mohit's withdrawal behaviour was increasing. His diet also reduced gradually, affecting his health. He had frequent attacks of cough, cold and fever.

One day, his parents had to go to their old locality for a marriage party. Mohit refused to go but it was not possible to leave him alone at home. So, they forced him to go with them. In the party, he occupied a chair and kept sitting quietly. Few of his friends came running. "Mohit...we heard that you have come. Why are you sitting here?"He gave an

I will take you to meet your old friends
P. Paul

artificial smile and said, "Not feeling well." But his friends compelled him to come to the dance floor and within 10 minutes, he was cheerful. He started roaming with his friends and talking about his new house.

Both parents were very happy to see him. His father overheard them talking: Mohit said, "Actually the house is nice. I have my own room. But I don't have any friends like you." When one of his friends said, "Why don't you come here every weekend?", he replied, "No, it is too far and it will be a problem for my parents. I hate that place. I don't want to go there. But I know if I tell this to my parents, they will be hurt. Moreover, it will be of no use. We have bought that house."

It was a touching moment for Mohit's father. He was able to know the cause of his son's withdrawn behaviour. When it was time to leave he called Mohit. There was a sudden change in Mohit's expression. He again became depressed. So Mohit's father went near all the children and said, "OK, when are we meeting next?" One of the boys said, "Uncle, please bring Mohit this Sunday." He replied, "Fine. I shall come here to meet my friends and Mohit would meet all of you. Will it be OK with you Mohit?" He was able to see the joyful expression on Mohit's face, although he managed to balance his excitement and murmured, "Yes".

Mohit's parents co-operated with him in managing the transition period. He felt motivated during the week waiting for the weekend and his motivation changed his energy level. When his mother took him outside to show him the brighter side of their new neighbourhood, he started talking to other children. She was friendly with the neighbourhood children and this made Mohit's interaction easier. This continued for two months, his father took him to meet his old friends every Sunday. One day strangely he said that he has promised some of his friends in the present neighbourhood to visit them on Sunday.

Now, they visit the old neighbourhood sometimes, not as an assignment but to maintain the old and sweet relationships. Mohit started recovering. He started loving the new playground with his new friends, he started loving his teachers and he started loving the walls of his new room. He became comfortable in this new place.

Summary:

Everyone wants a big comfortable house. In today's time, with prosperity everybody dreams of a big house. But for children, definition of prosperity and happiness is different. For them happiness is being able to maintain relation with friends. Change is as uncomfortable and threatening for children as for adults. So, when parents decide to change their house due to any reason, children's comfort level needs to be taken into consideration. Sharing and listening to their problems is very important. Moreover, the family which separates from a joint family needs to be more careful. The anxiety of separation with the family members with whom they feel attached may create serious behavioural problems, if not handled carefully. The child must be made aware that changing the place will not end the relation. There would always be the option of meeting the old family and friends in the weekends. Parents need to keep their promises. Gradually as the child will gain confidence in the new place, he/she would reduce the demand of going to the old place frequently. But maintaining the old relations is always necessary. The child would also learn the positive values of maintaining long-term relationships. It just needs a little effort. Even if children cannot express verbally, their behaviour shows signs of their needs which needs to be taken care of by their parents.

I will Not Listen to You!

Lakshay has become disobedient. When his parents try to correct him by beating him he looks at them with aggression. But he is now sure that he will not listen to any of their commands. They are quite upset with this behaviour. They failed in all their efforts to correct him. Even beating him does not yield any result. If they ask Lakshay to open the door for someone, he would simply say, "Why don't you go?". He has also become disrespectful. How can a boy of class V behave in such a manner? This is a shock for his parents.

Till class IV Lakshay was a quiet and obedient child. His parents were very proud that their child listens to all their commands. They also demonstrated this in front of guests. If Lakshay refused to obey any of their commands, they made sure that their prestige was maintained in front of the guest. So, they bribe him with something or threaten him that he would lose some of his favourite things. If these don't work, they never hesitate to shout at him in front of the guests. They just wanted to discipline their child in any way.

Like Lakshay's parents, most parents fail to see the difference between discipline and punishment

1. Discipline includes praise and instruction for the child on how to control his behaviour, while punishment is negative.

2. Discipline teaches children to live in a safe, civilised and harmonious manner with themselves and others, while punishment teaches what not to do.

I will not do the work. Do whatever you like.

3. Discipline teaches children to share and co-operate, to handle their anger and to feel successful and to be in control of themselves, while punishment controls children through fear and threats.

Lakshay was punished regularly under the pretext of the word 'discipline'. So, a point came when all these internal feelings had to come out. In the beginning, Lakshay remained passive and kept listening to all the commands with a pile of frustration in his heart. But now, this frustration turned from passive to aggressive behaviour. He could never express his frustration. Whenever he tried to do so, he was told to shut up by his parents because they feel that a child's expression of feelings means breaking elders' commands and breaking commands means breaking of discipline.

Lakshay behaved well with other people. He was considered to be a responsible child in the school. When his parents complained to the teachers about his behaviour at home it was beyond their imagination. They knew Lakshay was sensible enough to understand the difference between right and wrong. He never allowed any other boy to dominate anyone in school. They could not believe that he was disobedient at home.

The strenuous relationship between him and his parents was increasing day by day. It was difficult for them to understand his behaviour. They were upset and they took out all their frustrations on Lakshay.

What helped Lakshay and his parents?

Lakshay was disappointed with his parents' behaviour. Once when he went to his friend's place with his parents he was not willing to come back. He was touched by the affectionate behaviour of his friend's parents. But Lakshay's parents were adamant and when they started shouting at him he shouted back, "I hate both of you. You are not my parents." His mother broke down at this extreme reaction and his father shouted at Lakshay. Just then, his friend's father came running and said, "What is this Mr Chandol? He is a small child. Why are you behaving this way?" They all went inside and sat down to discuss the problem. Lakshay's parents shared how he is behaving these days, how much they love him and the amount of frustration which was getting piled up on them due to Lakshay's misbehaviour.

After listening completely to Lakshay's father, Mr Raichandani said, "I agree and understand what you are going through. But the impact which you are seeing today is not the poison of one or two days. This is accumulated poison. Most probably, you were not accepting the child's limitations. You did not value his mood. You always forced him to follow what you said. This has become too much for him now."

"Yes", Lakshay's mother replied, "But we did it so that he does not become disobedient. After all how can a child say 'no'?"

"Here is the mistake. He is a child. He is also a human being like you and me. He also has his own mood, own frustrations. We need to train him in such a way that he develops skill to manage his frustration. But the way you have pressurised him, his frustration increased and now this has turned to aggression towards you."

"So you mean to say that it is our fault?" Mr Chandol asked.

"No, your intention is not wrong. But the behaviour through which you wanted to fulfil your intention is damaging. Once you learn to direct your intention in a positive manner, you can see amazing changes in Lakshay."

Lakshay's mother remembered many instances where she was very harsh and pushed to get her own way. When Lakshay was very small, she remembered that she made her hold his ear and stand in front of all his friends and their parents just to prove how strong she is.

But it took a while to make Mr Chandol realise Lakshay's mental and emotional state. He did not say anything but his silence made the others realise that he was sorry for his actions.

When they reached home, everybody was quiet and Lakshay knew that he was going to be beaten up by his parents. He changed his clothes, brushed his teeth, and was ready for the beating. So he was very surprised when his mother came up to him and said, "Hey Lakshay!" She sat near him and said, "You wanted to stay at your friend's place? I am so sorry that we did not allow you to. I love you Lakshay. I understand you must be feeling suffocated due to our behaviour."

Lakshay was not able to believe what he heard. But he felt good. He did not say a single word that day. His father also showed normal behaviour. He was affectionate but did not discuss anything about the incident. This was again a surprise for Lakshay. Both the parents started thinking before speaking and started paying attention to his feelings. Things became better later on. There were moments when his parents were not happy with his behaviour. But they did not react and controlled themselves.

There were many instances when Lakshay used to shout and misbehave. They started training him to share his feelings not through his acts but through words. And it worked magic! The moment he started searching for words, his negative emotions vanished. Moreover, he found that he is being listened to when he is sharing his feelings through words. He became more expressive and even shared when he did not like any behaviour of his parents. As a result, he became more comfortable with his parents and, in turn, they were able to express and understand him better.

Ground rules about discipline were established beforehand so that no one is surprised by any new rule. The outcome was also decided. Thus, Lakshay knew which behaviour would result in what.

Gradually, a positive bond developed between Lakshay and his parents. They realised that the teachers were absolutely right about Lakshay being a responsible child. It was their over-anxiety which was creating a problem. In fact, his behaviour was the repercussion of their behaviour.

Summary:

Discipline should be a regular feature. Punishment should be meted out only when needed. If punishment becomes s regular feature, it will build up frustration. Moreover, frustration would lead to aggressive behaviour. To discipline the child, it is required to discuss about the ground rules. If discipline is imposed with force, it will have a negative consequence. Positive reinforcement focusing on the right behaviour of the child will enhance the disciplinary behaviour. If parents are not able to handle a situation well, it's better to think about an alternate way of handling, which should be practised next time. Human error may occur. But if we learn from our errors and rectify next time, the error will never recur. After all, parenting requires experimenting with things which works for the child. So, parents can learn many things. The most important thing is that expression should be a regular feature of the family. Freedom to express feelings should be given to each member of the family. After the feeling is expressed, negative comment should be avoided. Acknowledge the feeling and then, share other possibilities.

20

I Don't Want to Eat

Nine-year-old Shivam is a fussy eater. Everyday his parents have to struggle to make him eat something. He only likes to eat fast food and cold drinks. As a result, he is getting obese. It takes around two hours for Shivam to eat. His parents forced him to eat healthy food, but he landed up being sick. At the end, there was no choice other than providing him with what he wants to eat. But the problem occurred when doctors strictly instructed them not to provide him with any junk food since he also developed breathing problem because of his obesity. He will not eat at all if he is not given the food of his choice. When his parents tried to make him understand about the benefits of healthy food he quietly listened to them.

But when food was served he said, "I will not eat gourd. I will eat maggi."

"What? Till now you did not understand what the doctor said?", his father asked.

The argument went on for a while. Then, his father had to apply force and so he said, "You will have to eat this food. Otherwise, you will not get up from the chair."

His father went away but had to come back as for one hour Shivam did not take a bite. He used all his threats to make him eat. He ate few bites but with tears in his eyes.

Both parents were exhausted with this way of taking care of Shivam's eating pattern. He started having vomiting attacks. But they became too harsh and forced him to eat even if he vomited. They finally realised that this will not work and they need to search for something different for a long-term impact.

Most parents would be able to relate to this problem since there are many children who are fussy eaters. Many parents depend upon teachers to develop proper eating habits in the child. But teachers fail to do so.

What helped Shivam and his parents?

This realisation that force will have a negative impact helped them to experiment with some other method. They discussed with different people who had grown up kids as well as who had small kids and enquired about different strategies which might work for their child. This effort helped and they started applying the various ideas systematically.

First, they started maintaining a regular time schedule for eating. They found out a time when the child was not very tired as well as when he is moderately hungry. This helped not to upset his appetite.

Second, his mother took special effort to present the food in a more attractive manner for him.

Third, he was allowed to have choice one time a day. But the choice was based on options given to him. This helped Shivam to know his limits as well as have the enjoyment of choosing the food he liked. But once a week, he was also given the liberty to take food of his own choice. This was "his day" and he eagerly started waiting for this day.

Fourth, his mother started including him during her cooking time. This worked very well. She conveyed that Shivam has prepared the food. So, he was eager to get appreciation from others and he himself had no choice but to appreciate the food after eating.

Fifth, they started making the 'eating time' more enjoyable and interesting. They started discussing topics which was interesting. They changed their earlier habit of eating after his eating was over. Now they all eat and chat together. Shivam listens to stories told by his parents. In this manner, a great feeling of belongingness was created along with a change in his eating pattern.

Sixth, parents started establishing good examples themselves. They started discussing about what they will not eat as it is not healthy and what they would eat. This discussion took place in Shivam's presence. They started sharing about their wishes to eat different kinds of food but also the will power not to eat junk food. His father or mother said, "You know I want to have a burger, but I will control. I will not eat. I know I can control. If Shivam can, I too can." These kinds of statements helped him to stick to a healthy eating pattern.

One last but most important step taken by his parents was that they got engaged in outdoor games with the child. This helped them in two ways. First, it helped to exert the child physically. He got tired as well as hungry. Second, this helped to develop a bond with the child. It was a 'fun time' for all of them.

Summary:

Parents need to follow a holistic approach while dealing with children's eating problems. They need to be creative. There are many children who develop faulty eating pattern due to some psychological problem. So, the child's mental health needs to be taken into consideration. Apart from that, engaging the child in any physical activity, interesting story or chatting with him/her would be of real help. Creating a strong emotional bond is very important as force does not yield any long-term benefit. The child may eat, but may get sick. Presentation of the food may create an impact. Parents may try various methods to deal with the eating problem of their children. At the same time, they need to keep their patience.

21 What do You Know Other Than Beating Me?

Sunny studies in class two. He is smart, but overactive. He can do his own work himself – arrange his own book rack, clothes rack, serves the family members with bread-butter, polishes his shoes, helps mother in her work, helps father in his work. But he becomes overanxious when he wants to do any work himself. He will not let anyone do the work. When there is some hurry, it becomes difficult for mother to allow Sunny carry on with any work. This makes Sunny upset, he starts irritating and then his mother can do nothing except giving a slap to deal with his over anxiousness. She feels guilty about her behaviour. But she realises that when she has a lot of work, she cannot bear the self-work tendency of Sunny. She could feel that he has become very upset with her and keeps distance from her.

One day Sunny said, "Mamma, you only know to beat me. I will never talk to you." This sentence shook her. She understood the pain but was confused. How can she change her own style, if Sunny does not become calm?

Most parents feel guilty after hitting the child unnecessarily. When they are unable to deal with the temperament of the child, they deal with them with their physical power. Rather it would be better to say that they are unable to deal with their own temperament and make the child the victim of their own negative emotions. They are angry with someone else but shower their anger on the child, as they are unable to vent it out on the right person.

This is what happened with Sunny's mother, too. She also said "sorry" to her son many times. This is positive but carries no meaning if repeated several times. Sunny also mentioned, "Every time you beat me and then say sorry. No need to say sorry." Sunny's mother tries to explain in variety of ways: "Why don't you listen at one go? Why do you force me beat you again and again? I remain in hurry and you just don't listen." Sunny replies in frustration, "Can't you just make me understand in a low voice?" He is correct but at that point of time, she is so anxious and in a hurry that she just needs a trigger to burst out her irritation and he becomes the scapegoat.

She also tried to emotionally blackmail her son by saying, "Yes, I am a bad mother. You will see that I will be sick and die soon." Sunny replies, "Mamma you tell lies. You have said this many times." She is shocked to hear this.

This is another mistake which parents commit. They start emotionally blackmailing the child by threatening them that they would die. This can cause severe damages. There are few children who start feeling insecure. Some children may start following the same approach in later stage as they find it to be the best approach to gain sympathy. Many children start taking this statement casually and start thinking their parents to be "liars". So the child's respect for the parents deteriorates.

Thus, all efforts of his mother went in vain as she was unable to handle her son during this small moment of crisis. The tragedy is that such moments of crisis came every day. Every day, she was in a hurry when Sunny wanted to do some work.

What helped Sunny and his mother?

Sunny always wanted positive reinforcement. As he always had a feeling that he does not behave well, he goes to temple to pray to God.

One day he asked his mother: "Mamma, when God listens to you?"

Mother replied: "When you ask for something with full dedication."

Sunny: "But why doesn't God listen to me? I always pray to Him to make me so good that everyone calls me a good boy."

This brought tears in her eyes. She tried to explain, "No Sunny. God has listened to you. You are a very good boy."

Sunny: "No. I am not. If I was, you wouldn't beat me. Teachers would never give me punishment."

Mother: "Sunny, you are very good. Perhaps we are not as good as you are."

She was trying different ways to deal with this little kid so that he does not grow up to be harsh but she was unable to get any help.

One day, Sunny took a shoe box. Mother asked, "What are you going to do with this box?"

Sunny: "Mamma, I will make it my good behaviour box."

Mother: "What is this good behaviour box?"

Sunny: "Whenever I will behave well, you tell me at the end of day and I will put one slip in it. At end of month, I will check how many slips I have got."

Mother: "That is a great idea." She thought this way Sunny will remain calm.

The next day, when she went to the park, she realised that she herself, and not Sunny, needs to have the good behaviour box.

She came home and said to her son, "Sunny, will you put one slip for me too in the box for today, if you feel that I behaved well?"

and this is yours... the way you greeted the guest
Mummy, your good behaviour of today.
GOOD BEHAVIOR BOX

Sunny: "What? Your slip? Will you also play this game?"

Mother: "If you like it."

Sunny was excited and said, "Oh yes! But what shall we do after a month with those slips?"

Mother: "We can change each slip into one rupee each and buy fruits."

Sunny: "Yes, and give to poor children on the street."

Mother: "That is why you are my role model."

Sunny: "Mamma, what is a role model?"

Mother: "It means that I want to be as good as you are."

Sunny: "Mamma, you are already good."

And the 'good behaviour' box turned to be of great help for Sunny's mother. Every time there was a crisis for her, she said quietly, "Sunny, I know that you will understand. O.K., you do this work, fine?" Sometimes, she had to be firm by saying, "This is not the way Sunny. I don't expect such behaviour from you." This statement gave a 'feel good' factor to Sunny. He started thinking of himself as a good boy who is expected to behave in a certain way.

Every evening, they both discuss about their behaviour and added two slips for each of them (on one was written S and on the other M). Sunny's father was extremely happy to see such a beautiful relation building up between the two of them. In fact, this positive attitude spread and he, too, got the bonus of such positive behaviour at home.

Summary:

Children are very sensitive. They understand things more than adults can imagine. They realise when parents scold them because of their mistakes and when they burst on them because of their own frustration. So, parents need to take care of them with special care and concern. Every child has his/her natural behaviour pattern. So, we need to accept the basic nature of a child and then try to mould it in the best possible way. Natural behaviour will have some positive outcome at some place. If we constantly see when and how the behaviour is creating a negative impact, this will suppress the natural behaviour and thus damage the personality of the child. So, parents should not suppress the child's natural behaviour, but shape it in a positive manner with their own positive behaviour pattern. Moreover, based on our judgment we cannot declare that someone's behaviour is wrong. It may be that we are not able to handle it effectively. So, a reality check is needed.

I Hate to Lose

Ten-year-old Sharmishtha studies in class IV. She is very smart and outgoing, but cannot take any loss easily. She breaks down if she loses. She should not lose any argument, any game, and anything in her life. She becomes very anxious before any competitive event. Her anxiety shows on her face and behaviour. She will rub her palms or walk fast from one place to another. She cannot sleep for the whole night after the event. The problem does not end here. If she wins, she is overexcited, but if she loses, she starts doing research on how the judges or teachers were partial. If anyone favours the judge's or teacher's decision, she becomes her enemy. For one week she keeps on crying. She would not eat food; even if she eats, she would create lot of fuss with her choice. It becomes difficult to handle her irritation for a week. Parents too get frustrated due to this behaviour of Sharmishtha.

Fear of failure amongst children has become a very common problem in every family. Due to this problem, children are losing initiative and exploring new horizons. They try to be comfortable in their own comfort zone. The definition of losing has been attached to unpopularity, unattractive, poor, or being powerless. It injects the feeling that one time failure means failure for whole life. This is a perception which gets injected in the child's system.

Whenever Sharmishtha used to appear for any competition, she used to get one statement, "Remember you have to come first." When the competition was over, her parents were disappointed to find Sharmishtha lose.

Children are able to sense disappointments. Sharmistha got to know that winning or losing has something to do with her self-image.

I should never lose.
For me there is no failure: only success and learning
REPORT CARD

She accepted winning as a pride but losing as hurting and self-damaging. Being very attached to parents, children start feeling that their action has caused sorrow to the parents. Thus, they start avoiding many competitive situations so that their image remains intact. In the process, they lose many opportunities.

Sharmishtha lost her grandmother whom she was very attached to in the last seven years. During those years, she never missed any opportunity to listen to stories. Although all members of her family managed to deal with the crisis, it was difficult for Sharmishtha. She used to wake up at night crying for her grandmother. Could this be the reason? Has that relationship loss transferred to other areas?

Her mother agrees that she is anxious about Sharmishtha's result, whether academic or extra-curricular. So is it a mixed impact? We need to look at all the possibilities which might have caused the problem.

Reasons for not accepting loss may be listed as follows:

1. Any relationship loss.
2. Over-anxiety of parents towards winning.
3. Cribbing or disappointment after the child loses.
4. Linking any loss with worthlessness of the child.
5. The child's own self-expectation.

There can be many more reasons which can be added to the list depending on the child's situation. With Sharmishtha, it was both – relationship loss as well as over anxiety of parents. She was otherwise confident and energetic. But of late she has started developing a blaming attitude which could be the result of the fear of loss. She wants to save her self-image and finds blaming to be the best means to do so.

What helped Sharmishtha and how?

Sharmishtha was helped by her friend indirectly. Once she was playing carom with one of her friends named Ananya and, as usual, was anxious to win. On the other hand, Ananya was relaxed. There was a point when Ananya was about to lose. Sharmishtha was over-excited.

Ananya maintained her calm and said, "It's O.K. Good Sharmishtha, you are playing well." Sharmishtha replied, "Yes, I always play well." Sharmishtha's mother was standing near and was listening to their conversation and observing their behaviour pattern. Sharmishtha won the game. But Ananya was relaxed. Sharmishtha's mother called Ananya and said, "Are you feeling bad? Don't feel bad. It's OK. Next time you will positively win." Ananya calmly replied, "Aunty, I am not feeling bad because I learnt few things from Sharmishtha." That was surprising for her. She was so worried with her daughter that she called up Ananya's mother asking about her behaviour who said that Ananya was praising Sharmishtha's way of playing. Sharmishtha's mother could not believe that she lost but was still praising Sharmistha, without blaming her.

She decided that she had to meet Ananya's mother. When they met, there were few things which Ananya's mother said which were extremely useful for Sharmishtha's development.

Ananya's mother: "First thing which I do is that I promote her participation in any event."

Sharmishtha's mother: "I do that."

Ananya's mother: "Yes, I agree. But hope you don't add the winning factor. Hope you don't say that she has to win."

Sharmishtha's mother: "But I have to say that to motivate her!"

Ananya's mother: "Here is the mistake. Once you are stressing on her winning, she is missing out on the enjoyment. She needs to enjoy the process of participation and learn from the experience."

Sharmishtha's mother: "Yes, I get it. I think I over focus on her winning."

Ananya's mother: "Yes, over focusing on winning will move the focus from energy on participation. And ultimately, participating well will lead to winning. If the child is anxious about winning, this will create a negative impact on performance."

Sharmishtha's mother: "I get my mistake. Now tell me what to do if she loses?"

Ananya's mother: "First tell me what you do when she loses?"

Sharmishtha's mother: "I start by cribbing on the mistakes she had committed. I shout at her sometimes when I had put in lot of labour on her preparation."

Ananya's mother: "According to me, this is the second mistake. What I do is that I discuss on what she enjoyed and what she learnt. She never gets a chance to think about losing. Even if she loses, we discuss on some part which she enjoyed. She now comes up with number of aspects of enjoyment. Thus, she is learning to inject into her system to enjoy the process of participation and increase her energy level to improve upon her performance."

Sharmishtha's mother: "But that is difficult. I feel frustrated and angry when she loses. After all I have put in lot of effort. How can one be so artificial?"

Ananya's mother: "Here you need to change your thinking system. It is difficult but you need to work on yourself first. If you are putting your effort, your child is also putting her effort. The effort the child is giving will keep on reducing if you focus on negatives. She will avoid participating to avoid your negative statements."

Sharmistha's mother (with anxiety in her voice): "Yes, it is happening!"

Ananya's mother: "Why not you try for 21 days? It is said that it takes 21 days to form a habit. Try and then let us see whether it works. If it does not work, there is no negative impact."

Sharmishtha's mother was convinced but was doubtful about her own practice. She was scared whether she would be able to practise the new way of behaviour. But she experienced the positive feeling in Ananya's interaction pattern. So she thought that it was worth trying.

Initially, it was very difficult, but she tried hard. She forced herself to be positive without nagging. She managed to do it with some difficulties. But there was change in Sharmishtha's thinking. She started feeling relaxed. Her mother was able to sense the relaxed state. Many times, she came and hugged her mother and said, "You are the best mamma of the world." Sharmishtha's mother was able to sense that her daughter is feeling comfortable. She realised that she had imposed too much pressure on Sharmishtha.

Days passed by. And it worked. Sharmishtha's mother and Ananya's mother became good friends. The "carom game" turned out to be a great blessing for Sharmishtha.

Summary:

Children are not born with fear of failures. It is we who inject this fear within them. It is very important which statements we use when a child steps into some event – whether we are positive or negative, whether we are focusing too much on winning or also encouraging the child to participate. The more he/she participates, the more will be the chances of winning. Even if the child loses, he/she needs to be motivated for his/her participation. The learning part needs to be focused on irrespective of whether the child wins or loses. Thus there will be no storing of "failure" in the child's memory. In the long run, it will be useful for the child's overall development. The child would learn to face any difficulty with a smile on his/her face.

23

I Can Never Forgive My Mamma

Fourteen- year-old Namita has become extremely aggressive. It is beyond her mother's control to handle her. For every statement her mother says, Namita has something opposite to say. There is constant fight at home because of her. She has created her own boundary and seems to be satisfied in her own world. The girl, who was so chirpy when she was young, has become a very quiet child in social situation. At home, she is very aggressive. What happened to her? No one knew why she behaved in this way.

Namita was very friendly till she was nine and was studying in class three. Soon after that, her personality changed. It so happened that once she visited the house of some family friends along with her parents. Since her parents had to stay there for a while and she had to complete her homework, so they instructed her to go home with their friend's son. This was the biggest mistake in her life. When they reached home, this bhaiya whom she really admired sexually abused her. She was shattered. He was her role model but he became a villain for her life.

When Namita shared this incident with her mother, she showed a very casual attitude. Namita wanted support and concern. In return, her mother replied, "From now onwards don't cling to any guy. You always cling to boys."

She was blamed for everything. Her parents maintained cordial relation with the other family and spoke politely to the boy. She spent nights crying. She stopped sharing anything with her mother and went into her own shell. Her life changed completely. She started hating herself and her mother. Guilt entered her mind. Even

Rapport building time

her mother mentioned that it was her fault. So now, whenever she goes for family functions, she remains in her own shell. Aggression piled up in her but she was not able to share. She considered herself weak and helpless to express her aggression. So, she remained quiet all these years. But now that she grew up, she started feeling that she can express her aggression. Things became worse for her mother when she turned from being quiet to being aggressive.

Gradually, Namita developed an intense migraine problem. But she never had the desire to share with her mother. She tolerated it quietly. But now, she is detected with some neurological disorder. This was the time when doctor wanted to talk to the family. The doctor shared that she must be having acute headache. "Oh no!" her mother replied. The doctor had a small talk with Namita and got to know about her headache problem. The doctor was surprised to find that she shares nothing with her mother.

This was an alarming situation. There was something wrong, the doctor realised. So, he wanted to give some time to Namita. He realised that the psychological aspect needs to be dealt with to deal with her neurological problem.

What helped Namita?

Namita regularly visited the doctor. The first thing the doctor did was developing a rapport with her. He wanted to help Namita come out of her shell. Initially the response was more of doubt with close ended answers of 'yes' or 'no'. She tactfully made several checks. The doctor was trying to check her mental state and she, in turn, was struggling to check his trustworthiness. It took two months for her to develop trust in him and she became confident that whatever she tells will remain confidential. This was the time when she shared her heart with the doctor.

The doctor became more of a father figure to her. She always had seen her father accepting whatever her mother said, either right or wrong. But she found her dearest doctor to be different. He tells her mother what she should not do. He disagrees with her politely when there is any need without ever hurting her mother's ego.

After a few days, Namita shared her childhood trauma with the doctor. She spoke about the sexual abuse, her mother's blaming attitude, her crying regularly at night, how she was not able to adapt to any social situation, her hatred towards her mother, her aggressive feeling towards her father, etc. It took four hours to share all her feelings. She kept on crying while she was narrating her feelings. Sometimes she was quiet. The doctor, in fact, allowed her to be quiet. He too remained quiet with her as if he sensed her feelings.

She said at the end, "You know doctor, my mother never served me food after my sister told her that I was sexually involved with my tuition teacher. But the fact was that he, too, tried to abuse me. I never learnt how to deal with these people. All these men are….." She stopped and again she continued with calm voice, "except you." She shared one dream with tears rolling down her eyes, "I just want my mother to hug me for at least two minutes with lots of affection in her heart. I want to feel her affection, doctor. I wish she tells me, 'Namita, I understand you. You are not bad. You are nice. You are good.' This is the only dream I have in life."

The doctor said nothing. He did not want to show her any sympathy. He wanted to make her confident and come out of her past trauma. But he also knew that it would be better if her mother did the same. So, he spoke to her mother. When he shared about Namita's feelings, her mother was shocked. She never realised so many things were buried in her daughter's heart. She shared that she did not mean to hurt her but she wanted her to be cautious and so she blamed her. She never realised how this blaming will take her daughter to her shell.

Now, there was a turning point in Namita's life. Her mother started talking to her heart to heart. She was at the top of the world. She shared all her problems she faced in the past. Her mother, a number of times, had tears in her eyes. While Namita shared everything she listened very attentively. Namita was able to sense her mother's love and she became extremely relaxed. A complete catharsis occurred within her. She emptied herself of all her troubles. She cried for the last time. She never believed her mother could be so affectionate. When her mother apologised for not understanding her, she held her mother's hand and said, "I have got a lovely gift of my life from you. This is the most expensive gift I have ever received."

Namita's mother was in constant touch with the doctor. She started working on her guilt. One day Namita was in a sympathetic mood. She came up to her mother and said, "Mamma, why did it happen to me?" Her mother replied, "You know, Arthur Ashe, the famous Wimbledon tennis player, got AIDS due to blood transfusion during his heart surgery. But he never sympathised himself by asking why it occurred to him. He learnt to face the situation gracefully. He thought about the Wimbledon winning trophy which was in his hand. He said that he never asked God why he decided to hand over the trophy to him when there were millions of children who had started playing tennis. So, he faced this crisis gracefully." It made sense to Namita. Her mother then tried to explain with another example, "See, we need to see in a holistic manner. If you eat cooked rajma which is your favourite food, you like it. But what if I give you to eat raw rajma, then some water, then some salt, then some turmeric powder, then some spices, would you like it?" Namita instantly made a face and replied, "Of course no." Her mother replied calmly, "Same is for your life. When you see only bits and pieces, you may not like it. But if you learn to see life as a whole, you would enjoy the challenge it throws. Focus on your learning and also help others to learn from your learning experience. You know, Ashe set up an AIDS foundation. He became active in AIDS research at Harvard and the University of California, Los Angeles. He spoke to scores of gatherings on the nature of his disease, on race relations, on the lessons of life lived in the shadow of mortality."

Gradually, Namita became enthusiastic. She had the motivation to learn to deal with her life experiences in a positive manner. Her mother became her coach and guide. She was free to share her heart with her mother who became her best friend. Namita started meeting girls shared her experience. She started training youngsters on how to deal with sexual abuse. She became proactive instead of reactive.

Summary:

Sexual abuse is a sensitive issue. So, it needs to be dealt with a lot of sensitivity. It can cause a lot of emotional damage if not dealt with care and concern. The victim needs to get someone to talk to. Moreover, parents can take proactive steps to make the child aware of different precautions. As known people may create the problem, things can be very crucial. Communication skill is a very important component here.

24 I will Study Only When You Give Me a Robot

Prashant is very fond of battery-operated toys. He has lots of toys on his rack. Still he wants more of them. These days his problem has increased so much that it is difficult for his parents to meet his demands. Now, he has started imposing conditions for his every act. If he has to drink milk, then he would say, "First tell me that you would give me a remote-control car." If parents are not ready to fulfil the condition, they have to shout and make him ready for the task. He is now nine years old, studying in class III. When he finds himself not to be so powerful as compared to parents he accepts their demands with irritation and aggression.

It is surprising for parents from where do children learn to put forward conditions. For some children, this becomes a habit pattern. How to deal with these children becomes a big trouble for parents.

Some parents follow a bouncing back policy. For every condition of their child, they present another condition. The result is aggression and no fruitful solution. "If you do this, you will not get that", "If you do not do this, you will not get that", "If I do this, will you give that?" these statements start ruling the relationships. Generally the sentences roam around this framework with "this" and "that" changing.

But the main problem is, we always find short-cut solutions to deal with symptoms and rarely try to find out the root cause of the problem. If we really look into the cycle of these conditions, we realise that it started from a very young age, may be even when children were not able to speak fluently. How? Let us find out looking at Prashant's case.

The lesson of conditioning started when Prashant was two years old. When it was time to sleep, Prashant's mother used to say, "Sleep fast otherwise guard will come and take you away!" So he understood that to avoid the guard, he needs to sleep.

One day Prashant wanted a dress for himself. He did not get a proper response of whether he would get it or not. His mother replied, "OK, first complete your milk, then we will see." There was a chance but he was not sure whether he would get it if he finishes the milk? There was slight amount of anxiety. So, Prashant started asking his mother, "Will you give me the dress if I finish the milk?" Mother replied, "I said I will see." Prashant's anxiety increased. He now became more assertive to have a clear answer. He said, "No, I will not drink until you say whether I am going to have the dress or not." This was the way in which Prashant learnt to put conditions.

Children learn very fast through observation and imitation. So, Prashant started imitating his parents. Parents were not even aware about the negative impact of their actions. They realised only when things took a concrete shape and it started harming them.

Parents unknowingly train children to do things with conditions. So, in order to change the children's habit, we need to change our own habit pattern. It is difficult but this is the only solution.

In Prashant's case curative action was required. Prevention is always better than cure. So, it is always better to convince the children

I love helping without any condition
FILE

without conditions as a preventive measure. But for curative measure, we need to proceed further.

What helped Prashant and his parents?

Once there is proper awareness of the problem, there is a solution to it. Some parents find the solution instantly and some with trial and error method. With Prashant's parents it was more of trial and error method.

First, they tried to use force. His father started beating and shouting at him. He used statements like, "OK, so you will only do the work if we give you a robot? Let me see how you don't do the work. Till you do not do the work, you will not have anything to eat." If Prashant still managed to stick to his demand, he did not take much time to hit him harshly. But things became worse. Prashant became more aggressive.

Prashant started getting away from his parents. He started saying to relatives, "What can my father do other than beating me? And my mother has only one thing to do: Complain to my father." This statement was shared by Prashant's grandmother which brought a big shock to his parents. They were shaken. Now they had to choose another method of handling Prashant's problem.

Grandmothers always prove to be the best counsellors. So, they took her advice. She asked them to be firm while he puts any condition, but not to bounce back with their own conditions. Parents were apprehensive. They were doubtful whether this will work or not. Prashant's grandmother first asked them to come out of their own doubts because if we are trying to solve something with doubt in our mind, chance of success becomes less, On the contrary when we approach any problem with confidence, chances of our success increase.

First they worked on their confidence level. Second, they tried to get rid of their habit of putting conditions for every work. It was the first day and a big examination for parents. His mother asked, "Have you completed your homework?" Prashant replied, "No, first you play with me." It was a difficult situation. She assertively said, "It depends upon you when you finish your homework. I am not going to say anything."

It was a shock for Prashant. No conditions! Now what to do? He thought of his teacher's punishment if he did not finish his homework. He came behind his mother and said, "Please play with me. I will finish my homework." She maintained her calm and assertive voice and said, "Prashant, I will play any time with you and I love to play with you, but not with the condition of your doing your home work. I do not appreciate your statement. If you wish, you do your homework." Prashant tried to convince more. But she replied, "I will not talk to you at this moment. Give me some time to be quiet." Prashant could not bear it anymore. He went to his room and started doing his homework. His mother then came and held him in her arms and gave a sweet kiss on his forehead. He was happy. So, he again said, "Mamma, please play. See, I am doing my homework"

This is the tendency of children. When you start loving them, they would put some conditions or demand. Prashant's mother knows this trick of her son. She replied, "So you want me to go back to kitchen. I wanted to sit with you as I liked your behaviour." She took a turn when Prashant caught hold of her *dupatta* and said, "Sorry mamma. Come sit." It worked.

And yes, it will work. Prashant's parents were determined to get rid of this behaviour. It was challenging but they were prepared to take the challenge.

Summary:

It is difficult to handle children's demands and conditions but we need to know that children learn to put conditions by observing parents. Parents put forward various conditions thinking that this would make the child do what they desire to do, but they are not aware of the negative impact which may occur at a later stage. Children learn very fast. So, parents need to be aware of every step they take in disciplining the child. Once children form the habit of putting conditions, it becomes difficult to handle their tantrums. But there is a solution to every problem and the solution to this is to change the parents' habits. Once parents stop putting conditions, children learn to be responsible for their own behaviour and outcome. So, parents need to learn to be supportive, rather than being conditional.

25

I Want to Burn My Hair

Mrs Kuldeep Kaur was very satisfied with her son till one incident. Her eight-year-old son, Harpreet, has numerous qualities. He is bright in his studies, helps his mother, listens to others, etc. But one day, Harpreet came back from school and immediately went to the kitchen where his mother was working. He instructed his mother in a commanding tone to switch on the gas burner. When she asked him why he wants her to do so, he instructed her to do as he is saying. Mother felt that he must have learnt some experiment in the school and he wants to show her. As she lighted the gas burner, Harpreet opened his turban and untied his hair. He almost threw his hair on the gas burner when she dragged him scolding, "What stupidity is this?" But Harpreet broke down by shouting, "I hate my hair. My friends tease me that I am a fool. They say that I am born fool as I am a sardar." Mother looked at her child. She realised that many a times Harpreet mentioned the urge to have his hair cut but she never realised the reason. She always taught him about their custom and stopped Harpreet from saying all such impure things.

Harpreet was teased due to his turban, because of his being a sardar. Some children are being bullied by various other words like, 'motu', 'kalu', 'chimpu', 'chhotu', 'lallu', etc. these children may show that they are normal but internally they are not. Their self-esteem gets hurt and it becomes difficult to cope up in a group.

Shashwat, studying in class VI, shared with one of his teachers, whom he admired a lot, one such thing. He told that he is planning a fight to take revenge on Aman who keeps on teasing him by saying that his body stinks and he does not take bath. When asked how he is going to do that, he confidently mentioned

Motu!
Motu!
Motu!

that he has good relations with some boys of class VII. He has already made a deal with those students.

The deal is that he would give a party to those VII class students and they would beat Shashwat outside the school gate when the school is over. The case was handled as Shashwat mentioned the issue with his teacher. But there are very few students who are lucky to have a teacher whom they could share their heart with!

Parents of children like Harpreet and Shashwat do not want themselves to be involved with these petty matters. But these are not petty matters for these young kids. These children are bullied in groups which hurt them even more. They develop a sense of rejection which directly hits their self-esteem. There are very few who bully but no one in the group oppose this. The reason being, they feel safe that at present someone else is the target. They fear that if they oppose, they might become the target. They find the best way to have safety is to support the person who is bullying. Thus bullying becomes more of a game and enjoyment. But the sad part of this game is that one has to be the victim.

Is the problem only with the victim or also with the person who bullies? This is an important question. Training is needed not only for the victim but also for the person who bullies. The main reason behind bullying is to fulfil their power motive. It may also be that they are trying to fulfil their need for importance in this way or these children may observe such kind of behaviour in their family. If parents throw sarcastic remarks on each other, children learn to let down others through teasing. Moreover, this person may lack self-esteem. So, he might put on a mask of confidence by bullying. There may be sign of depression or dissatisfaction in some area or the other. But this person who bullies does not know what the victim is undergoing internally. The frustration accumulating internally may burst out any time, but how it would, is unpredictable.

Training for both the bully and the victim

Some important tips for handling the bully:

1. Parents need to be aware of the home environment. They need to check whether there is respect in the family. The child should feel emotionally secure in the family.

2. Child should be trained appreciation skills. Let the child know that socially competitive individuals are trained to give genuine appreciation. Parents need to appreciate the child when he/she appreciates others.

3. Parents should immediately check any of child's sarcastic remark in the family. For e.g. if a child tries to let down the younger brother by saying any of his own pet word like *'lallu'* parents may quietly say, "You look better when you talk politely. Can you show me how you can speak this sentence politely?" Just mentioning that the child is using bad words is not sufficient. Demonstrating the right sentence is very important.

4. Parents can play game of "communication". There can be dialogue exchange between parent and child. Some situation can be presented like, what to do when you wish to praise someone. Then, let the child demonstrate different ways to do so. Thereafter, parent can also be a part of the game. This would create emotional bond with the child as well as train the child in communication skills.

What helped Harpreet and his mother?

Harpreet's mother was very upset and was not able to understand how to wipe out the feeling of inferiority from his mind. She praised him a lot to make him realise about his positive traits. But Harpreet wanted his hair to be cut. He was sure that his friends would tease him by saying, "See... *sardar* is coming", "Harpreet, it must be 12 o' clock for you, isn't it?" Such sentences were rotating in his mind. He constantly asked his mother why he can't have hair cut. He will still have respect for his religion in his heart! Why his hair cut will be an insult to his religion? She was not able to convince Harpreet. But the point which she knew was that Harpreet needs to learn coping skills with such bullying students. The solution lies in how he would deal with peer group.

Mrs Kuldeep was indeed very anxious. She went to his school and spoke to the class teacher who was very supportive. The class teacher handled the situation tactfully. She took a class on 'bullying and teasing'. First she herself disclosed how she was teased when she was a child. Once she disclosed her own experience it was very easy for the children to open up. Each and every child of the class mentioned how they are being teased. Harpreet also mentioned his own point.

Then she came up with the feelings ('how it hurts'). First she mentioned that when she used to be teased, she had difficulty to concentrate in her studies. She told them how she felt humiliated. When she was expressing her feelings, all the students were quietly listening to her. It was as if she was opening their feelings from within the hearts. The children who used to tease Harpreet were more alert. After allowing them to express their feelings, she came to the disadvantage of teasing. Most of them expressed about losing friendship. Many moral issues also came up. When a few students mentioned that they have learnt that it is not good to laugh at others she took this opportunity to explain how we get back what we give. She asked the students, "What we get from one seed of mango? Do we get one mango and one leaf or many mangoes and many leaves?" All the students raised their hands. She gave opportunity to a so-called naughty student. The student said, "We get many mangoes, many leaves and shade." The teacher appreciated the student and linked it with behaviour. She replied, "Absolutely right. Same happens with our behaviour. When we hurt others, we get hurt in bulk. In some way or other we will be hurt. But if we do well to others, we will be treated well in bulk. When we are small, the best way to do well is by words. We can appreciate

others. When someone is teasing, we can bring some positive point of the person being teased. This would make you a hero of the group."

Everyone was quiet in the class. The teacher broke the silence by asking, "Do you want to be a hero or heroine of the world?" There was a loud yes.

She ended the class with this positive note. In the next class she continued the same session. Now she focused on what to do when someone is criticising or teasing. Most of the children shared aggressive ways of handling. Now she focused on what would be the disadvantage of this aggressive mode of handling. She explained, "If we are aggressive or trying to take revenge, will we be able to remain good ourselves?" They replied, "No". She mentioned how she handles when someone teases her, she said that if she does not like, she just keeps quiet and looks at the person teasing her without any expression. She gives no reply. Most of the time she mentioned that she has seen positive outcome. The person teasing does not find any enjoyment. Then, she personally talks to the person who teases by saying, "I did not like the way you behaved. It hurts me as I believe you to be a good friend of mine." She mentioned that this sharing also helps. But in the sharing she never blames or criticises. She also mentioned that sometimes she smiles and moves out of the scene.

It seemed as if the students were finding great relief. Harpreet came home and shared with his mother, "Mamma, you know there is no harm if someone teases me. I will just smile and go away. You know if I am good, I will get many good things in life. I feel I have got this favourite cycle because of my being good. I feel the toys which I have must be because of my good deeds."

Mrs Kuldeep was very happy to see the change in her child. She knew the reason. She was very thankful to the class teacher and wished each student should have such a teacher, who not only focuses on completing the syllabus but also on various life skills which are important parts of education. She added, "Harpreet I feel I have you as a son just because of my good deeds." Harpreet looked with a smile. His eyes reflected lots of confidence.

Summary:

Teasing/bullying is very common in peer groups. It may not be harmful for some children, but for some, who are sensitive, it may cause serious problems. These children need to learn how to deal with this problem. They need to be trained on various response patterns so that the words used in bullying do not enter their internal system. The first thing required is that when the child faces any teasing situation, the parents should never ignore by saying, "Don't think about these things. They are not good boys. You are a good boy." By just telling not to think about those hurting words or insulting situation will not stop the thinking. If children are hurt, they would think till they do not know how to deal with the situation. The best way to train them is role modelling. Let the child play the role of the child who is bullying. Parents may play the role of the victim. Thus the child will learn about various response patterns. At least the child will mentally prepare himself/herself to face such bullying situation. Moreover, parents should frequently discuss how to handle such situations. Parents should work on the child's self-esteem. Genuine praise and appreciation is a must to enhance self-esteem. As children who are victim tend to be sensitive they should never be corrected in front of others. When any visitor comes, it is better to mention the positive and omit the negatives. Negatives should be observed and be worked upon when the child is alone.

Correction also should be with modelling. Let the child demonstrate what could be other possible ways of behaving. This would also make the child mentally prepared to face the situation with an alternate positive behaviour. At the end, it is important to mention that dealing with bullying is a joint effort. Parents, teachers and other members of the society can join together to check the bullying tendency in the child.

The bully should also be handled with care and concern. Their self-esteem should not be hurt. If they feel insulted, their bullying tendency will increase rather than decreasing. Talking positively is the only solution.

Few more books on Parenting

A Parent's Guide to Child Care

–*Dr. Suresh Keshan*

150/-

Children are both a delight and a liability for their parents. The birth of a child evokes mixed reactions from the parents because child care is viewed more as an onus than a pleasure.

Dr. Suresh Keshan, a practising paediatrician, enumerates easy ways to handle your responsibility. In the book **Child Care**, he makes parents and would-be-parents realise the fact that planning for a baby is a lovely experience. He instils a sound confidence in them. This makes them realise that they are doing the best for a healthy baby to grow to their fullest satisfaction—both physically and mentally.

The book also provides remedies of common problems related to:

- Neonatal care
- Breast-feeding
- Common childhood diseases
- Immunization
- Growth and development
- Schooling

Mama, I'm Hung

–*Juhi Aggar*

Rs. 88/-

Mama I'am Hungry. As a youn mother, how often you hear thes words... For mealtimes can be th most challenging time for any mothe and feeding an infant or toddl calls for more than just preparin any ordinary meal. It require imagination to prepare meals th are both tasty and nutritious. Sinc the health and growth of your chil depends largely on nutritious meal what, how and when to feed yo child is of special significance. Th infant's diet also calls for a slo transition from mother's milk to liqui diet, from liquids to semi-solid from semi-solids to a soft diet, final culminating in normal family meal The book outlines this transitio with meticulous care. The recipe chosen are wholesome, covering variety of food in order to develo their taste buds. They are easy t prepare and based on homemad ingredients. Alternatives are give at the end of each recipe. Not onl does this book provide guideline for lifelong healthy food habit developed in the child's formativ years, it ensures delicious meals fo the child with a growing appetite.

Postage: Rs. 15/- per book

EW MORE books ON PARENTING

Raising a Daughter In 21st Century

–Rupa Chatterjee

Rs. 80/-

The Joy of Parenting

–Sangeeta Gupta

Rs. 96/-

ıe mother of two daughters, author has used both, her own erience and suggestions from rs, to give valuable insights bringing up a daughter in 21st tury India.

has not only attempted to ılight the problems of bringing a daughter today, but also tried how how these can be tackled how the best of our traditional es can be combined with ent requirements to bring up a -adjusted daughter.

book contains time-tested sane suggestions and reliable ommendations, with insights paediatricians, psychiatrists, hers and other experts, and serve as an effective guide for mothers, particularly first-time ıers.

pered with numerous first-on accounts, **Raising a ghter in 21st Century** India can e as a handy guide in moments ying tension, while dealing with teenage daughter.

In the days of yore before the advent of television, the Internet and other extraneous influences, parenting was a simple task, especially in a joint family milieu. Today, bringing up children is a more arduous, complex and delicate task. The common-sense guidelines in this book will ensure you maintain just the right balance between firm and flexible parenting, as per the attitude, aptitude and ability of your child.

Besides negative influences from the electronic media, children are especially vulnerable to peer pressure. How you handle your children during their formative years can make all the difference between having courteous, well-adjusted children who respect elders, peers and friends or being saddled with ill-mannered kids who are a law unto themselves.

The book covers all the important aspects of childrearing to help you become a role-model parent.

Postage: Rs. 15/- per book